My [illegible] With an Oyster

and Other Stories of a D.C. Girl Discovering Chesapeake Country

M.L. Faunce

New Bay Books

My Date With an Oyster
by M.L. Faunce

Editor
Sandra Olivetti Martin
New Bay Books
Fairhaven, Maryland
NewBayBooks@gmail.com

Design by Suzanne Shelden
Shelden Studios
Prince Frederick, Maryland
sheldenstudios@comcast.net

Cover Photo: Oyster Shell, *by Suzanne Shelden*
Interior non-captioned photo credits: page 181

A Note on Type: Cover and section heads are set in Adobe Handwriting (Ernie). The text font is ITC Bookman with subheads in Apollo MT.

Library of Congress
Cataloging-in-Publication Data
ISBN 978-1-7348866-2-7

Printed in the United States of America
First Edition

DEDICATION

In memory of my mother Florence Louise, and father, John Patrick Faunce, my sister Joanne Knotts and brother Pat Faunce ...

For Shelley Fletcher, my partner; and for my niece Janet Knotts, whose love and support sustain me ...

And for Kathleen Wilson, my longtime friend ...

For my brother Brian Faunce and my niece Julie Louise Shirley and their families.

My special thanks to Sandra Olivetti Martin, for her editing that rescued my writing, and for making publication of this collection possible through New Bay Books; and for our friendship.

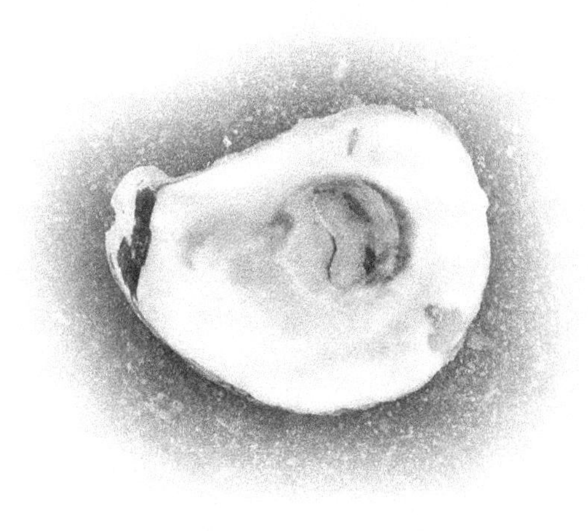

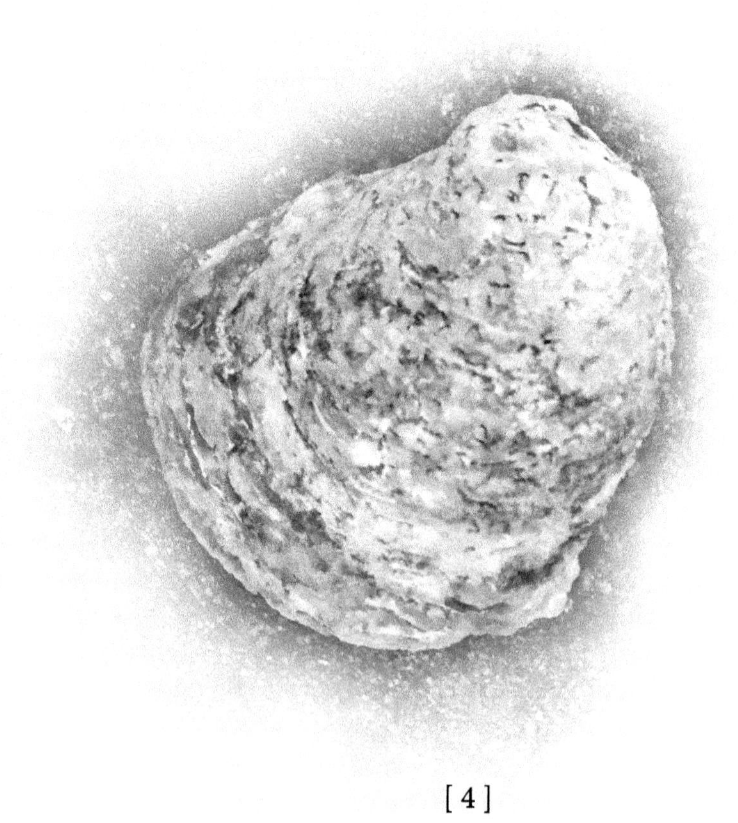

FOREWORD

There is a story behind this book. It is a two-part, twining story. One part of the story is its author's explorations of her land of childhood fantasy—as a property-owning, voting citizen. The second part of the story is how an upstart weekly newspaper authorized her to go anyplace, do everything, speak to everybody, ask most every question.

M.L. Faunce took Chesapeake Country to heart when she made it her home, enchanted by its natural beauty, mores and quaint local culture. A post office, a library, Elks and Moose clubs, many churches but more bars, shambling Smith Brothers Lumber (a store for all hardware needs), a port for working and pleasure boats, the Shady Side Rural Historical Society, fields of tobacco, feasts of crabs and oysters —and all of that keeping close company with the expansive Chesapeake Bay.

The Churchton Post Office, she would write on May 18, 1995, *was one of my many pleasant surprises as a newcomer. The postmaster and staff were not only efficient and helpful but also had a sense of humor. When a clerk wheeled to my car the numerous boxes of gifts my sister sent to me from Alabama, he heaved a sigh of relief because he now had "room for the Christmas mail for the rest of Churchton."*

That bylined story reached thousands of readers four years after M.L. had brought home, from that very post office, week after week's editions of New Bay Times, "the paper committed to the Chesapeake." For all those weeks, we—for my family and I were that paper's founders—had lured M.L. with stories of Chesapeake Country, from the Annapolis Capital region through rural Southern Maryland to well-preserved Solomons Island and the Patuxent River.

M.L. courted her way into New Bay Times, for she —though an irrepressible storyteller—did not call herself a writer. Not yet did she know our secret, hers for the asking: We wanted to hear the many voices of Chesapeake Country.

A college teacher of writing for many years, I ran a teaching newspaper whose open-sesame was curiosity. I couldn't teach you curiosity, but I could teach you to write.

M.L. eased into our pages: A farewell to tundra swans in April; in June, a couple of reflective essays, including the above Postal Discoveries. By November, she was all in, contributing two, sometimes three, even four stories a month. Caught in a symbiosis that was hard to escape, M.L. kept up that pace for a half a decade, and for six more years she contributed amply.

She'd bring me a story, and I'd suggest two more after fine-tuning the first. There were so many good stories demanding to be told, and M.L. was what an editor loves most: eager to chase them all.

For all those years, M.L. was our indispensible utility player, willing and able to pitch, bat or catch in whatever role the paper needed. She wrote stories for our charming kids page, Not Just for Kids; she wrote news stories; history stories; personal essays; profiles of local people Black as well as White; features stories; seasonal observations; dog stories; land stories; sea stories; creature features—and topped all that off with letters to the editor, often under the pen name borrowed from her mother: F.L. Collins.

Along the way, M.L. the storyteller became a writer who told you not only the who, what, where, when and how of every story but also why it mattered. To achieve those answers in her reporting, she covered the waterfront, quite literally, traveling hundreds of miles in Bay country, seeking out experts who were born to their subject. Her stories were encyclopedias unto themselves.

Journalists from across the country recognized her achievement, awarding her feature stories first prizes two years running, and one year the grand prize for science writing in competition including *The Washington Post and Baltimore Sun.*

From such documentaries, M.L. would rotate to a personal essay straight from her heart to yours.

This anthology collects two-dozen of those short personal and seasonal essays plus six feature stories, all on vanishing icons of Chesapeake culture. The feature stories, all snapshots describing a time that was, are briefly updated to 2021.

Read them to feel the beat of a human heart and to tour world-renowned Chesapeake Country just past its tipping point into a more anonymous future.

Sandra Olivetti Martin

Sandra Olivetti Martin
New Bay Books Publisher
Fairhaven, Maryland

Oyster shucking in the 1990s.
New Bay Times photo.

Table of Contents

M.L. catching a good late summer haul
of fat crabs on the Wye River, c. 2002. *Faunce family photo.*

Introduction

My writing life came to me when I discovered a weekly newspaper called New Bay Times. I had recently moved to the small community where the paper was published, and its news and stories of Bay life from Annapolis and along the Western Shore of the Chesapeake captivated me.

As a long time Congressional staffer for a U.S. Senator from Alaska, I had just returned home, after several years of living in the Last Frontier, to care for my mother. When my mother passed away and I needed the solace of change, I made a move back to the place of frequent childhood's trips to the beach with my mother and father and siblings for explorations of the Bay and its tributaries from the summer cottages of family.

Those early memories of a child raised in Washington, D.C., crabbing and fishing and boating with my cousins were the stuff of dreams.

Intrigued by the stories in New Bay Times, I thought: Maybe I can write about Bay life, too. I sent a first piece to Editor Sandra Martin—and she accepted it!

So began a dozen or so years of joyful writing. I loved the column Who's Here, later changed to Earth Journal, that evoked all that was unique about Bay country—the nature, the culture, the history, the community, news and activities and all the seasonal changes, where the fish were biting, what's happened to the once-prolific oyster that filtered the Bay for a centuries, the lives of watermen and future of skipjacks that sailed the Bay.

And so I wrote and wrote and wrote. Essays, and commentary and features about the changing Bay and changing times, challenging times, the people who make their living from the Bay, those who come to enjoy and treasure it.

Bay Weekly, as New Bay Times became, also gave me the opportunity to write about my family, and for that I am eternally grateful.

Later the award-winning weekly captivated an amazing following. And I had the pleasure of writing by whim and assignment. Here you will find some of those stories.

—M.L. Faunce, Gulfport, Florida

- one -

Seasonal Reflections

January

Savannah's kindergarten birthday party. *Faunce family photo.*

January
Earth Journal

Winter Came Late to Chesapeake Country

Winter finally dawned in late January. The horizon, stacked with hues of slate grey, rose and aqua, is layered as thinly as a Lady Baltimore cake. A winter sky at last, I think, as temperatures dip to the norm.

But what is the norm and how do we measure it? Depends on where and the expectations of whom, of course. Now global warming adds its cachet. In our mid-Atlantic region, this period was the warmest on record. The warmest ever.

In my neck of the woods, winter is signaled by the arrival of tundra swans that migrate here from the Arctic around Thanksgiving. This year, the flock on my creek is diminutive. Perplexed enough by the tepid weather, they compete for food with droves of descending resident Canada geese.

Quince blooms in my yard. Cherry blossoms parade their petals around the Tidal Basin in nearby Washington. In plant-hardiness zones, oh, the times they are a-changin'. We've moved a whole zone warmer.

The crape myrtle that spill like summer fountains in Chesapeake gardens are no longer on the northern edge of survival. That's because Maryland has shifted from a cooler Zone 6 (average low temperature of -10 to zero degrees) to a warmer Zone 7 (average low of zero to 10 degrees), according to the Arbor Foundation's just-released Hardiness Zone Map for the country, updated from the United States Department of Agriculture's 1990 map.

Amid more sober subjects in print news and on the air these last two months, headlines blared: *Record Temperatures; El Niño; The Year Without a Winter; No Ice Fishing*, Please. Up north, polar bears are said to want for ice, with floes too few and too skimpy to support their hefty weight. Used to a rich diet of seal, they are bereft as their hunting grounds melt into seas. Across the globe, our Russian friends gripe and groan for what's missing in their lives, the deep annual freeze that justifies an antidote they pronounce *wodka*, the antifreeze that takes the edge off of endless northern nights.

The winter norm for my Hawaii-based family, now newly minted Virginians, used to be picnics on the beach. Six-year-old niece Savannah has only seen snow once: That white winter arrived by dump trucks. Intent on giving their kids a white Christmas for once, U.S. Marines at Kaneohe Bay shoveled it into a small mountain.

Here, Savannah dreams of snowflakes on her tongue and eye lashes, as new snow boots from L.L. Bean stay boxed. On her January birthday, a day that peaked at 73 degrees—up from the more typical 43-degree weather—she left home clad only in a polka-dot bikini to greet kindergarten friends at her swimming-pool party.

The winter of our content, a winter of flip-flops and shorts and outdoor BBQs, may be over.

I, for one, am happy to see the return of the norm, of a winter sky with stars at night and a kaleidoscope of color by day. A little snow wouldn't hurt.

Think of the polar bears and a family from Hawaii. The crape myrtle will be fine.

—February 1, 2007

Reflection

Counting Gains and Losses

After some 12 years of living by Chesapeake Bay in Churchton, I find myself marking days not by jotting things down in a journal but by noticing things returned.

On a recent cold and dark Saturday morning with the window ajar, I lay in bed listening to the quiet. No whine from a neighbor's heat pump, no motorcycle cranked up by another (your neighborhood, too?). So when I heard a faintly audible sound that wasn't coming from my sleeping pup, I sat up and took notice. Drifting over wetlands outside was the unmistakable soft *hoot, hoot, hoot* of an owl I hadn't heard in years.

Other things returned this last year, too. The northern bobwhite for one. Gone for years, then *zot!* on a summer day, the clear crisp notes of this quail-like bird pierced the air like an arrow. A box turtle visited on the Fourth of July. Later, a praying mantis fixed its spindly legs to the window screen at summer's end. The Carolina wren I wrote about three years ago that roosted in a little hanging basket by my front door reappeared this winter with a mate. At least someone got lucky. I wondered if it was the cotton balls I stuffed in the basket for her comfort that did the trick.

In Bay Country, we can count on many creatures to return regularly: tundra swans; bluebirds, in my yard at least; cardinals most definitely—by dawn and by dusk they visit each day. A cast of characters too numerous to mention—hummingbirds, kingfishers, dark-eyed juncos all return to us in multitudes. Read the poignant little book, *I Heard the Owl Call My Name* by Margaret Craven, and you'll understand this richness of nature. How when creatures are lost they are gone forever, and when we take the time to know them, they are always ours.

Deer hurtle over backyard fences as if at a track meet, heading for the Bay. No deer Olympics lately, except on the roads. A rooster that announced every day the first few years of my residence by the Bay crows rarely nowadays. What became of the "Lost Goat" sought in the sign posted at the head of Franklin Manor Road this fall is anybody's guess. I failed to note the phone number (of the owner, not the goat), though I remain intrigued to this day. Can anyone enlighten? Still, for me, the things that have returned far outnumber those that haven't.

I know that not everything comes back to us, really. We suffer losses both large and small. We forget and are sometimes forgotten ourselves. Still, much comes back to us: Not always in the form we recognize; not always the object of our desire—but in the spirit hidden deep in our hearts. When we have taken the trouble to observe nature around us, and listen close enough, we hear it call our name.

—January 30, 2003

Stewin'

Is This Our Bay Oyster's 11th Hour?

First Place and Best of Show Maryland, Delaware, D.C. Press Association

From Maryland's rural Eastern Shore to the more populated Western Shore, from Baltimore to beyond the Beltway, when the air crisps and the leaves turn, Marylanders want oysters.

Despite dwindling supplies and dismal forecasts, oysters are sought and found. Oyster roasts reign at volunteer firehouses in Southern Maryland. Stand at the bar in historic Middleton Tavern at City Dock in Annapolis or at Happy Harbor on Rockhold Creek in Deale and you'll discover the most popular bar food is oysters, not nachos. Not content with a raw oyster on the half-shell, legions of oyster lovers slurp down shooters, oysters served with cocktail sauce and a shot of beer on the side.

Prefer your oysters cooked? Happy Harbor serves Oysters Southern Maryland, Oysters Karen, Oysters Friendship, Oysters Ohio, Oysters Caribbean, and Oysters New Jersey, in addition to oysters five or six traditional ways. Across the Bay on the Eastern Shore, Harrison's Chesapeake House on Tilghman Island and Harris Crab House at Kent Narrows both offer Friday-night buffets laden with oysters.

At Thanksgiving, Maryland dinner tables will groan under turkeys stuffed and dressed with oysters. On Christmas Eve, Mary Watters of Churchton still plans on serving her family's favorite baked oyster recipe. Around the state, Marylanders by the bushel will stew up steaming bowls of the beloved bivalves from now through April.

Where are all those oysters coming from? Surely not from our oyster-depleted native waters.

Breaking the Law of Supply and Demand

Degraded water, sedimentation, loss of habitat, over-harvesting and disease have ravaged the Chesapeake's legendary shellfish. The same problems make the future look as bleak as the present.

Chesapeake Bay, our back bays and ocean waters used to teem with native *Virginica* oysters. No more.

Numbers tell the sorry story.

We're a long way from the harvest we once had, even in the 1970s and '80s. Over two million bushels of oysters were annually harvested before disease mortality struck in 1987. A century earlier, a whopping 10 million and more bushels of oysters were harvested annually.

Last year's harvest was an all-time low of 26,495 bushels, according to Chris Judy, Maryland Department of Natural Resource's man on shellfish. To put that figure in perspective, it's only half the previous all-time low, a then-low 55,840 bushels harvested in 2003. In that company, 1994's previous all-time low of 79,618 bushels seems abundant.

This year, Judy imagines a new record will be set. "It's been a slow start to the season, the worst ever in terms of boats and people working," he said. "We were used to seeing about 100 boats working; now we see only a couple of dozen."

What happens to an industry when demand outstrips supply—and there's no more supply to be had? What does scarcity mean to watermen who should be at the top of the food chain? What about the shuckers, who would shuck if they could shuck?

What do you do when your menu calls for oysters, oysters and more oysters?

"We try to have Chesapeake Bay oysters for our shucking contest and raw bar sales," said David Taylor, administrator for the hugely popular annual St. Mary's County Oyster Festival, where tens of thousands of oysters are consumed each October. "We haven't had all Maryland oysters at the festival in six or seven years. Last month, we had oysters from Chester River, but also from New Jersey, Virginia and the Carolinas."

This year was tighter than ever, for neighboring oyster waters were suffering their own problems. "Everybody was in a pinch because the hurricanes closed the Gulf Coast to oystering, and when no oysters are coming from the Gulf, it puts a squeeze on other supplies," said Taylor.

"There was talk of bringing oysters all the way from Washington state, but that proved unnecessary."

As at the St. Mary's County Oyster Festival, the majority of oysters sold now come from out of state. Most oysters you're eating this season in Chesapeake Country come from the Gulf Coast, according to Karen Oertel, whose family packing plant, W.H. Harris Seafood in Grasonville, shucks the bulk of local oysters.

A Good Shucker Is Hard to Find

When you're talking oysters, you could get to thinking of the old song about foot bones and knee bones and thighbones. Oysters, too, are connected. They support ecosystems underwater, on the water and on land.

Thus before you can eat an oyster, somebody's got to shuck it. That's true whether oysters are served raw on the half-shell or processed for sale to restaurants, food processors, groceries or you and me.

Eight men and six women competed in this year's National Oyster shucking contest at St. Mary's County Oyster Festival in Leonardtown. Some shuckers came from other states, including Florida and Washington. Like oysters, Maryland shuckers are fewer nowadays. Most can't make a living shucking.

At this year's competition, Samuel Fisher was the exception. The agile Fisher, of Ocean City, has practiced his craft for 30 years, 20 of them at the Crisfield oyster-shucking house Metompkin Bay Oyster Company. He moonlights at two Ocean City restaurants, The Embers and The Bonfire.

"There are not many like him," said Bud Harrison of Harrison's Chesapeake House. Steeped four generations in waterways, Harrison laments that shucking is a dying art.

"Not a lot of young people are learning to shuck," he said. "I have eight shuckers who have worked for us more than 25 years."

The youngest is Charmaine Lake, 36, of Hurlock, who's been shucking since she was 12, Both her mother and father were shuckers, Harrison said. The oldest is Woodland 'Woody' King, 91, of St. Michaels. "He's shucked for us ever since my dad opened the oyster house in 1965," Harrison said. At Harrison's Friday night oyster buffet, you can see Woody shuck those small, salty, round oysters from Tangier Sound.

Harvey Linton employs 11 shuckers, all older people.

"Those good people are dying off," he said, so when the going gets tough, he, three of his four sons, his wife and his daughter will shuck. "It's a family business," he explained.

At Metompkin Oyster Company, Brenda Thomas counts "maybe 30 shuckers. The younger person is not learning and the older ones are dying off," she said. "It's a dying skill."

When no locals can do the job, Metompkin imports workers from Mexico on H2B federal work visas.

The training grounds for shuckers are also in decline. Only about six packing houses remain in Maryland, according to seafood marketer Noreen Eberly, of the Maryland Department of Agriculture. That's down from two dozen in the 1980s and about 100 in the 1890s.

Oysters come direct from the Bay to Bud Harrison's family's shucking house on Tilghman Island, enabling the family restaurant to serve Chesapeake oysters. *Photo by Sandra Olivetti Martin.*

Trading in Maryland's Last Oysters

However scarce, Maryland oysters can still be found—if you know where to look for them.

Levin Faulkner Harrison IV, called Bud or Little Bud after his father Captain Buddy Harrison, said oysters served at the family's Chesapeake House on Tilghman Island are all local. Points of origin differ from week to week; at the end of October, the oysters came from the Deal Island-Tangier Sound area of Chesapeake Bay.

"We try to serve something a little more saltier for half shell stock, and this small round oyster can't be beat," said Harrison of the bushels shucked for waiting diners.

Chesapeake House serves 20 bushels of oysters on a typical weekend. At about 220 oysters per bushel, that's a lot of oysters on the half shell. To supply their needs, Harrison buys from watermen, who are independent contractors, selling at whatever price the market will bear. Price drives everything, but buying for cash often wins out close to the weekend said Harrison.

Oysters direct from the Bay.
Photo by Sandra Olivetti Martin.

A different Bay oyster is cooked at Chesapeake House (and sold by the pint and quart when supplies allow). The difference shows. The Chester River oysters harvested by a couple of hand-tongers early this year Harrison described, with no exaggeration, as "big as my hand." Trouble is, the oystermen were tonging in only about eight bushels per boat each day.

"We're hoping things will improve with the skipjack dredge season, which opened in the upper Bay November 1," Harrison said.

The old local skipjack-style of working sailboat is about as rare as the oysters they catch. Because skipjacks are at a disadvantage against today's gas and diesel-powered oyster boats, state regulation allows a motorized push boat to assist the larger craft two days a week. To further level the playing field, skipjacks are the only oyster boats allowed to dredge for oysters.

On the Thomas Clyde, Captain Lawrence Murphy is now harvesting about 75 bushels a day, working his skipjack under motor two days a week and sometimes a third day under sail if conditions are perfect.

Bud Harrison called Thomas Clyde's catch "very nice oysters, a little bigger and cleaner because they're being dredged out in the middle of the Bay where it's a little fresher, from a bottom that has always been dredged, so the oysters are spread out and can grow bigger."

In Crisfield, oyster packer and shipper Harvey Linton also swears by the Maryland oyster. "It sells itself," he said, "not only by name, but also by the quality and taste.

Harris Crab House shucks and serves local oysters, but supplies are not enough. Karen Oertel, one of the family, wants to see non-native *ariakensis* oysters planted in the Bay.
Photo by Chris Judy.

"I don't buy oysters from Texas and Louisiana," said Linton, who has worked the water for 33 years—"since I was a kid" before turning seafood wholesaler. "All my seafood comes from this area."

Linton also sells the salty Chincoteague oysters to restaurants from Baltimore to Rehoboth Beach, from Washington to Deale. He ships all over the U.S. and the world. Wholesale and retail sales over the internet accounts for about 35 percent of his business, Linton says.

Deep connections to the water and established relationships with suppliers keep both Harrison and Linton in Chesapeake oysters.

THE SHAPE OF LUCK

Both oyster purveyors like to think they're finally getting a break.

"It looks like we're going to have oysters this year," said Harrison. "Out of nowhere, we have a lot of small oysters, one and a half to two inches. Lots of bars covered with them."

That good fortune he ascribes to forces outside human control: the hurricanes this year and Isabel last year may have helped.

"There's an old saying that a bad wind always does someone good," Harrison said. "Flow is good, and in another good year they will be harvestable if [the rampant oyster diseases] MSX and dermo don't kill them. We will be watching them very close. They survived this August and September, so I'm kind of optimistic that we have a natural oyster set coming back."

"Less bad water this year," is how Linton described the shape of luck. "July and August are usually hard on oysters, but this year fresh water helped flush everything out," he said. "Fresh water helps oysters more than anything in the world; it makes them fatter because they grow faster."

Drought years that began in 1999 have been hard on the oyster harvest, for they've brought higher salinity with consequent high levels of disease and mortality. Karen Harris Oertel, of the Harris clan's Harris Crab House at Kent Narrows on the Eastern Shore, called the flow of fresh water a "reprieve" for oysters and for watermen.

Chris Judy, DNR's man on oysters, expects this year's harvest to be the lowest ever. *Photo by M.L. Faunce*

DNR's Chris Judy agreed that a little good luck has finally come Chesapeake way. "With fresh water flow over a very large area of the Bay, oyster mortality has declined. Mortality has lessened, survival is better," he said. "But," cautioned the scientist, "it's too little, too late."

"Even good news is way too late," he said. "You're still at rock bottom. We have a terrible situation. Next year the diseases may return."

Thus Harrison and Linton are anomalies in today's oyster market.

Metompkin Bay Oyster Company in Crisfield runs truer to form. The family business—owned by I.T. 'Ira' Todd, and sons Casey and Mike Todd—has shucked and packed Maryland oysters for 55 years. They still shuck roughly 30,000 bushels a year. But Metompkins now gets most of their oysters from the Gulf.

"There are not a lot of Maryland oysters right now; some, but not enough, not even enough to shuck," said the company's Brenda Thomas. "We sell all the local Chesapeake Bay oysters that we can get. It's pretty sad.

"Good night," she said, watching the clock count down the native Maryland oyster.

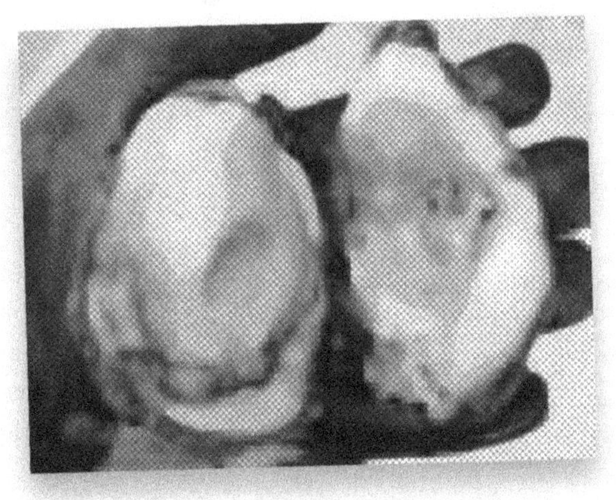

A healthy reserve oyster, left,
versus one blighted by disease.

How to Shuck an Oyster

Some say shucking is more finesse than brawn. Watching an expert shucker, you'll know why it's a dying art. If you enjoy the tangy taste of a raw oyster, here's how to begin with finesse.

Shuckers wear heavy rubber gloves for good reason, and so should you. Hold the oyster cupped gloved palm of one hand and your oyster knife in the other. Oysters have sharp, brittle ridges, and oyster knives, though rounded at the tip, are thin and lethal. Handle with care; no death grip needed.

Run the knife around the lip of the oyster. Insert the knife, as my dad used to say, "at about 4 o'clock." With a twist of the knife, pry the top and bottom shell apart, being careful not to spill the precious liquor. Then slide the knife below the oyster to cut the muscle free from the shell.

According to Harrison, "a real oyster shucker can cut into the bivalve, slip the knife under the shell and cut the heart away from the bottom portion, which relaxes the muscle, so both the top and bottom shell will separate—all this without tearing the meat."

Harrison said he is glad to demonstrate this dying art and willing to arrange small tours, which will surely whet the appetite for dinner at his family's Chesapeake House.

BEYOND LUCK

Water quality means a living to Larry Simns. Charter fishing captain and president of the Maryland Waterman's Association, Simns believes only cleaning up the Bay, starting with sewage treatment plants, will restart the clock for the native oyster.

"Until we're willing to do what it takes to clean up the Bay," he said, his kind has to look past the native oyster to survive. "We need a different oyster to bring back the Bay," Simns said.

Harrison thinks so, too. "The implementation of the *ariakensis* is important," he said, "if for nothing else than the help it can give to clean up the Bay. If we have that, in connection with a natural set, it may help jump-start the native oyster harvest."

To his way of thinking, a new oyster can't but help the Chesapeake's natural oyster. "Even if eventually the *ariakensis* is harvested," he said, "the natural oyster will make more money. They're two separate products, but people will want the natural oyster."

Sterile ariakensis, a naturalized Asian oyster, is growing in Bay and tributary waters in both Virginia and Maryland, in studies that could lead to its introduction in the Bay, eventually even as a reproducing, reef-building transplant. *Ariakensis* has been used to clean up the water in other areas of the country and world, and it seems able to resists the diseases MSX and dermo.

Under instruction from Gov. Robert Ehrlich, Maryland's Department of Natural Resources looks to making a decision on introduction this year. Many scientists are urging slower speed and greater caution. Thus the National Academy of Sciences recommends at least five more years of study before it's decided whether the Asian species will help or hurt the Bay. But for Oertel, as for many in her industry, too much time has already been wasted.

"*Ariakensis* has been in the Bay 14 years and came out of years of testing by the Virginia scientific community. The native and non-native oyster can live side by side," she said. Sanctuaries of native oysters are another means to the same end: revival of the bivalve, the Bay and an industry.

"I don't care if we ever harvest the oysters" growing in sanctuaries, said Harrison, who explained that they're needed "just to start to clean up the Bay." Since 2000, Maryland's Oyster Recovery Partnership has planted some 400 million oyster spat at 38 locations, comprising 23 sanctuaries, eight harvest bars and seven managed reserves.

Sweetening the Pot

Some of these cosseted oysters are destined to fatten Maryland's lean 2004 oyster harvest. In the Chester and Choptank rivers, October ended with the first harvest of oysters planted in 2001 in three of those spots.

"The special harvest day was aimed to give a boost to the annual yield for our Maryland watermen," explained the Oyster Recovery Partnership's Tilly Egge.

Those oysters are as carefully bred as prize beef cattle or hogs. They're the progeny of natural native brood stock selected from cleaned bars to give the oyster the best chance to resist disease. For all the serious science by a boatload of partners, the goal of oyster recovery is basic: restore the health of the Bay and help the oysters to help fuel the economy of a historic Maryland resource.

In the short term, the 4,000 bushels expected to be harvested from the reserves may be as much as one-quarter of this year's full Maryland harvest, estimated at a lean 15,000 bushels. "For the oystermen, the reserve harvest may be the only break they get," Judy said.

So on October 30, a dozen or so boats worked the hot spot over Blunts Bar, a carefully tended reconstructed reserve in the Chester River. A handful of boats milled about over Emory Hollow, the other Chester reserve. Each harvester was allowed to catch 10 bushels. Both hand-tongers and divers went after their limit.

A tonger, balanced on the washboard of his workboat *Tammy* out of Bozman, worked all morning in a continuous bump-and-grind action, first squatting low, then arms pumping side to side. Finally, in a twist-and-shout kind of way, he stepped on a power assist and pulled the lanky, 20-foot, wooden tonging rake to the surface, dripping mud but holding oysters in the tines.

Hand-tonging is backbreaking work, and nowadays scuba divers outnumber the tongers. A buoyed flag flying from the *Jenny Lynn II* signaled that a diver was working the bar below the murky water's surface. Off the bar, he was chipping baskets of 2001 class oysters to be hauled aboard. On deck, a wire basket full of oysters and mussels spewed mud and spat while the family crew culled, separating harvest-size oysters from smaller fellows and empty shell.

The reef the oysters grew up on was artificially constructed, but nothing was artificial about the four-inch, disease-free oysters. Shucked, they were plump, full and glistening.

A second managed harvest came November 13, with a third planned just before Christmas. Any licensed oysterman who has paid an additional state permit charge can join in the harvest.

On October 30, Maryland Waterman's Association Simns returned to Harris Crab House at Kent Narrows to shuck some of the prized booty, which was destined for several area restaurants—among them Old Ebbitt Grill in Washington, McCormick and Schmicks in D.C. and Baltimore and Nick's in Baltimore—to promote local oysters. Simns allowed that sanctuaries and reserves could help the native oyster.

But it wouldn't substitute for cleaning up the Bay.

What's That You're Eating?

Where does your oyster come from?

At Middleton Tavern, chef Arthur Gross is responsible for the restaurant's oyster purchases.

"We don't get many from Maryland now. Most of ours come from Mississippi and Texas," he said. "They're really nice and closest to our local oyster. On an average weekend, we'll use 15 bushels in the shell that we shuck here. But for the oyster shooters, we'll use already shucked 'standards,' from the Gulf."

Gulf oysters are Eastern oysters, the *Crassostrea virginica* that we're used to and which were once so bountiful in the Chesapeake region.

At Happy Harbor in Deale, Barbara Sturgell gets her oysters "right out of the Bay." Four bushels a week of oysters in the shell are bought from Don Sheckells of Shady Side, who supplements what he can catch in the Bay with oysters he farms in the West River. Another eight gallons, from a supplier in Virginia, are harvested from the southern reaches of the Bay.

No longer are we that 'great shellfish bay' the Algonquin Indians called Chesepioc. Until we find the will and the way to clean up the Bay—and that may cost $28 billion, according to the latest scientific estimate—we'll continue to import our namesake product.

As we whet our oyster appetite on shooters, that's a sobering thought.

—November 18, 2004

UPDATE: 2021

Oysters continue to work for the Bay.

In the years after this story was written, Maryland has recommitted to restoring *Carassostrea virginica* as the Chesapeake's oyster. Working alongside Maryland Department of Natural Resources, the Chesapeake Bay Foundation and the Oyster Recovery Partnership, thousands of Marylanders are growing and planting oysters at their piers and in their communities. Thus in the wild, *virginica* retains a fragile hold on the Bay's bottoms.

Sanctuaries now help oysters recover. Oysters now live and grow unharvested in over 250,000 reserved Bay acres. Though with oysters so scarce, that's proving a hard line to hold.

The wild harvest of the 2019-2020 oyster season was 270,011 bushels, ten times the 2002-2003 harvest of 26,495 bushels. But watermen continue to lobby for more opportunity.

Aquaculture continues to grow as part of the oyster economy, adding more oysters to the water and harvest to the table. In 2019, 54,903 bushels of oysters were raised, either on Bay bottoms or floating cages, to harvest. Aquacultured oysters extend the oyster season as well as supplement the harvest, as they come to market all year long, not only in the winter months. They are also an ecological boon as they also work to filter the Bay.

Ariakensis oysters were decided to be a bad idea for the Bay.

Sandra Olivetti Martin

New Bay Books publisher

- two -

Seasonal Reflections

February - March

February Earth Journal

February Is Like a Box of Chocolates

I adore February. But then, a month when love is in the air, snow is (sometimes) on the ground and cherry pies are turning golden brown in the oven is hard not to like. It's a month easily identified on the calendar—though we now celebrate the birth of two great leaders under the generic name of President's Day. Meanwhile, a lowly groundhog gets called by his own name: Phil. And the shadow this small creature casts on the world sets the tone for the next two months, as the words of our national leaders begin to fall on deaf ears.

It's February and yet it is not. The month that promises an end to winter, and often delivers our deepest snows, has left us adrift this year in mild, wet wash. We haven't gotten the Big One this year that some thought El Niño would bring—nor even a little one. Our ground is as barren of snow as the trees are of leaves. Some hearts are content.

We are no poorer for this mild winter. A paucity of one thing often brings memories of the bounty or overabundance of another time. This year we can be almost smug when we remember the blizzard of '95 or the Ice Storms of '94—though living through them was more like a nightmare. Now, few creatures of the woods and field go unfed. And while we witness scandals in humankind, we know of no scandals in nature—unless it is the voracious squirrel whose wanton appetite exercises power over those lower in his food chain.

It's February, but fall-blooming cherry blossoms have this year bloomed right up to this month of our Founding Father's birth. It's certainly February in the acorns that now lie mounded and cracked open under the red oaks. The second month is here, when we feast and fete and fatten ourselves before entering the period when many will give up pleasures of secular life for the Lenten life and its promise of rebirth.

Daffodils are up a good three to four inches. The tips of tulips appear interested in joining the fray. The Bradford pear is losing the battle against the sun's warmth; its buds as fuzzy as the rabbits regularly venturing out of their underground caches. It's February and it's not.

Maybe February is like a box of chocolates: You never know what you'll get.

—February 5, 1997

Reflections

Transitions

Back in the early winter when the happy days of Halloween were but a memory, a plump pumpkin stood all by its lonesome propped on top a tiered wooden stand at Thompson's Farm Stand on Muddy Creek Road. Each morning as I drove to work, I glanced at the pumpkin that was not chosen for the short life of a jack o' lantern but remained to pass through the season as fields turned brown and trees lost leaves.

When Christmas came calling to the farm stand, the pumpkin was soon surrounded by balsam and spruce and pine trees, disappearing as holiday trimmings of rope and wreaths took their rightful place. Now, as the sun's rays strengthen, hinting of another season, only a Christmas wreath remains at Thompson's, tacked high on the side of an aging barn, testimony to the hectic holiday season we've now all but forgotten.

On Muddy Creek Road today, wind and rain and wet snow fly at the windshield as I drive pell-mell to our Maryland Capitol to a job at the General Assembly that races to its predetermined conclusion in April. No season, no life is without its transitions. They're the time that prepares us for what comes next and helps heal us from where we have come.

A neighbor who spied my vigorous yard raking on a recent blustery, bitter day thought me impetuous, perhaps, and said as much as I swept the yard clean of those nemesis sweet gum pods some call monkey balls. On cutting back drying Bay grasses to scatter like fronds of Palm Sunday, I liberated seed on which a family of cardinals soon fed contentedly.

We can find purpose as we flush away the debris, our healthy toil liberating us from the doldrums of winter as the Ides of March approach. But finding a nest in the bluebird box gave me pause and made me wonder: Was this intricate mass of grass and fine twigs the hapless result of poor planning by a bird last fall—or a new promise of what lies ahead?

If a new nest, was it a blue bird's that must be protected? Or was it that of a scrappy wren, which is less choosy and not at all threatened? As caretaker of the nesting box, I wonder what to do. So it is with affairs of the heart. We are not always certain of the outcome but by necessity make our choices, carrying on.

Transitions are like that, and late winter is full of them. Snow clings to the first blossoms of spring. Dreams overtake regrets. What we lament in winter becomes our second chance in spring. Transitions bring us a new day and a new us.

A Time magazine cover may have said it best back during the turmoil of election season. Framed and hanging on the wall in my computer room, it reads, "Yes, We'll Survive."

Both we and nature will, of course, survive—thanks to transitions and our need to carry on.

—March 8, 2001

March
Earth Journal

Longer Days, Shorter Daffodils

"This morning I had sun while reading the newspaper for the first time this winter and such a good feeling," my friend, Peggy, a lifelong Alaskan, exclaims by email. By March, even Alaskans start reclaiming their daylight by about five minutes a day.

For Alaskans like Peggy, the extra daylight in March "means a great new beginning," she says.

Up north, gardening season doesn't begin until well after Memorial Day, when there can still be snow on the ground and ice on the lake. So when the inner clock says it's time to garden, many Alaskans turn to their greenhouses to keep green thumbs in practice. "My tomato seedlings are straining toward the real light," Peggy says. The same light that's now shining in her eyes in the morning.

Here in Bay country, we're noticing longer days, too. Now, we can either leave for work in the daylight or get home before the sun sets.

My Alaska friend's enthusiasm got me looking around my garden to see which plants were heeding the call of all this extra daylight. My quince is blooming. Daylilies, in this mild winter, have kept their foliage full and green. Hyacinths are just emerging with color bordering on chartreuse. One sunny spot in my garden has tulips up several inches, while those in cold shade stay shy and sheltered beneath the mulch. Iris rhizomes are sending up wide-toothed leaves. But the daffodil is March's surprise.

A discovery in my own garden was reinforced as I scanned my neighborhood and walked toward the Bay. On a day winter returned, a cold wind from the north took my breath and pushed the water out several hundred yards into the Bay. Yet all along the waterfront, daffodil narcissus waved in the cold wind. Like the ones in my yard, this year, perhaps they should be called daffodil diminutive.

Everywhere I looked, hosts of foreshortened daffodils fluttered daring in the breeze. The closer to the Bay and cool water I got, the shorter the stalk, some only a few inches tall. Did the mild winter and late cold burst stunt their growth? Have the stately King Alfred variety so commonly grown here suddenly given up the throne to a little prince?

Since plants grow huge when Alaskan days grow long, I couldn't resist asking Peggy about her daffodils. "Oh, I never grow daffodils," she said, "they look so silly here when they come up in June and the rest of my garden is in full swing."

How are your daffodils sizing up this spring?

—March 11, 1999

Reflection: Women's History Month

Char or Chore, a Woman's Work Is Never Done

A while back, I read that female night custodial workers at the U.S. Capitol won an equal-pay lawsuit. The $3 million dollar settlement—the first-ever class action lawsuit against the Architect of the Capitol—was considered a milestone. The suit argued successfully that female workers were entitled to the same pay as male night custodial workers, who earned an hourly wage of $11.41.

Given the current state of our litigious society, the story may not have caught my attention, had not my Irish grandmother, Lillie Collins, worked at the Capitol as a "charwoman" some 60 years ago. She toiled at night cleaning offices—a job few of us ever notice unless left undone—in the same buildings where I later worked as a congressional aide.

In my grandmother's day, charing (the name originating from the Middle English chore) was women's work. My grandmother's pay, I learned from the Architect's archives, was an uncontested 50 cents an hour. Her job, secured for her by a congressman from Virginia, was a form of patronage.

During the day, the grandmother who died before I was born worked as a nutritionist for Visitation Convent, a private school for privileged young women in Georgetown. In her spare time, the skilled seamstress assembled dress shirts for a men's clothing company. She raised a family of nine, mostly on her own. Then times were tough, families were large and wages uncertain.

Today, women can be aviators and astronauts, administrators and architects, adventurers and artists. Some are in the same workforce as my grandmother. In my office building, they are rarely noticed unless you work late and see the empty boxes in the hallways on which we scrawl *basura* for the night custodial workers who have yet to learn English but know how to earn a living and care for their families.

What I know of my grandmother, I was mostly told: She had a fine sense of humor and deep pride; she was a wonderful cook, quick to set another place at the table.

Women are at the table now in all ways, making up half the work force. Competing, contending, connecting. Still, their work is never done.

—March 11, 2004

Wrangling Oysters out of Trouble

At Circle C Ranch, Aquaculture to the Rescue

First place Maryland, Delaware, D.C.
Press Association

Down on Circle C Ranch in St. Mary's County, Richard Pelz thinks he's got a pearl of an idea for bringing back both the Bay and oysters you can eat.

Time was when crushed oyster-shell roads sparkled in the sunlight leading to packinghouses along both shores and many tributaries of Chesapeake Bay. Now, wild oysters are nearly gone from river bottoms and Bay reefs, and with them much of the Bay's oyster industry.

At the end of December, 2002, Maryland's harvest was a record low 28,000 bushels, putting us in line for the worst harvest in history when the total is figured in March.

"Microscopic organisms have East Coast oyster production under their thumbs," said Chris Judy, Maryland Department of Natural Resource's man on oysters. The microscopic organisms of which he speaks cause the devastating diseases MSX and dermo.

It's so bad out there that some—scientists and watermen alike—have given up on our Bay's poor old Eastern oyster. There's even a substitute waiting in the wings. *Carassostrea ariakensis*, a non-native Asian oyster species that's won hearts in Virginia, seems to have all the good of its native American cousin with none of the bad.

Richard Pelz, left in overalls, is leading the effort to grow oysters at his Circle C Oyster Ranch in St. Mary's County. With the help of Paul Flynn, right, they grow oysters fast enough to outrace the Bay's oyster diseases. *Photo by M.L. Faunce.*

But not so fast. Not everybody's ready to throw in the towel on *Carassostrea virginica.*

Watermen, scientists, state legislators, nonprofit organizations and universities have just the first draft of a Baywide plan to restore our native oyster. Throughout Chesapeake Country, people are studying the plan as you read this story, to get their comments back to the Chesapeake Bay Program by January 15.

There's Hope in the Water as Well as on Paper

The Oyster Alliance—a joint outreach of the Maryland Sea Grant Extension Program, the University of Maryland Center for Environmental Science, the Chesapeake Bay Foundation, and the nonprofit Oyster Recovery Partnership—is working with Bay dwellers to nurture spat for sanctuary reefs where oysters would grow not to be harvested but to revitalize the Bay. That Alliance boasts 55 million oysters planted in the Bay and its tributaries in 2001—with higher figures likely for last year. And, down in St. Mary's County, Richard Pelz thinks he's got a pearl of an idea for bringing back both the Bay and oysters you can eat. He calls it oyster ranching.

Pelz's Pearl

A fisheries biologist from Ohio's gently rolling farmland, the bearded, ruddy-faced Pelz dreamed of fertile fields of oysters.

He searched the East Coast before settling on St. Jerome Creek, a five-fingered creek on the Bayside of the St. Mary's peninsula above Point Lookout. There, on what he calls the "best location in the nation for an oyster aquaculture activity," Pelz founded Circle C

Oyster Rancher Association, which is Maryland's leading—some say its only—commercial oyster-culture facility.

Why is this spot so promising? In the wild, oysters grow faster in salty water, but that's where disease and predators lurk. This creek is halfway up the Bay, where salinity is lower and the deadly oyster disease MSX can't thrive. Here "the only predator is the blue crab," said Paul Flynn, number-two man in a three-person team that operates Circle C. So far so good, but Pelz has more plans to speed his oysters along.

Wild oysters grow in reefs, living mountains that rise as new generations attach to the shells of their ancestors. Pelz farms his oysters on Floating Oyster Reefs, three-by-10-foot trademarked floats of white PVC tubing. Each reef is seeded with some 1,200 inch-long oysters, lashed to the reefs in mesh sacks suspended inches below the surface of the creek.

Water-column aquaculture, as Pelz's method is known, places oysters in a zone of food and oxygen where they can feast on the fresh algae that grow

Circle C's floating oyster reefs on St. Jerome Creek.
Photo by M.L. Faunce.

there naturally. Managed in this environment, Pelz said he's grown oysters from larvae to four inches in only nine months. By 18 months, they reach a jumbo six inches.

Secured to the 200-foot dock where he farms, each reef occupies only about 30 square feet of water space. On one-tenth of an acre of water surface, Circle C is farming a quarter-million oysters.

Paul Flynn with the floating reefs on which Circle C's oysters grow. *Photo by M.L. Faunce.*

AQUACULTURE RIDES AGAIN

At Circle C, Pelz has refitted an old idea for our times. Propagating and cultivating aquatic animals in a controlled environment dates as far back as 2000 BCE in China. Closer to home, Maryland was among the first states to recognize the value of leased oyster grounds.

As early as 1830, Merrill Leffler wrote in *Oyster Farming vs. Oyster Hunting: A Century of Conflict*, the Maryland General Assembly allowed citizens one acre of leased bottom ground for planting and growing oysters. But why take the trouble of farming when wild oysters seemed to be infinite? Leased bottom ground was used mostly for holding a catch of wild oysters until the market price was highest.

After all these years, oyster farming is still seeking its way in Chesapeake Country.

Raising oysters on leased underwater bottoms has never produced more than two percent of Maryland's oyster harvest, according to the Comprehensive Oyster Management Plan. Water-column aquaculture, Pelz's method, is still experimental. Most water-column aquaculturists are oyster gardeners, who grow a small crop to be seeded in sanctuaries.

Their successes are considerable. Consider, for example, what's been achieved by Chesapeake Bay Foundation's oyster gardening program.

"Initially, we thought we could recruit about 100 people per year," to be oyster gardeners, said Stephanie Reynolds, self-described "oyster wrangler" for the Foundation in Maryland. "In the past two years, it's been over 200 per year."

In Maryland alone, the Foundation trained 223 oyster gardening households in 2000. That's not counting schoolteachers who are gardening oysters with their students. Reynolds reported that citizens and students together planted 882,940 oysters on sanctuary reefs in Maryland waters in 2001. Since 1996, Maryland gardeners have raised half a million adult oysters for sanctuaries.

But back in the sanctuaries, those carefully nurtured oysters are vulnerable to the diseases MSX and dermo that, over the last 15 years, have killed oysters faster than nature or humankind can grow them.

But not faster, said Pelz, than he can grow them.

Will It Work?

Talk to different experts, and you'll hear different opinions about the likelihood of Richard Pelz's dream growing into a pearl.

The Maryland Department of Agriculture, according to Flynn, is "100 percent behind us."

Maryland's director of aquaculture development and seafood marketing, Noreen Eberly, did not go so far. She said her department "supports the development of commercial oyster growing."

Such activities, Eberly noted, "grow the industry as a whole and get people interested in the industry. They also mean we'll have more oysters in the Bay for both its health and for ecological benefits and to bring to market."

Marine biologist Don Webster of the Maryland Sea Grant Extension Program was more specifically enthusiastic. Developments in aquaculture make ours "one of the most exciting times to be here in the last half century," he said.

Webster envisioned oyster farms as safe haven from a disease that has devastated the oyster industry in Chesapeake Bay and its tributaries. Farmed oysters, he hopes, would indeed grow fast enough to reach harvest before microscopic oyster predators kill them.

Others are not so optimistic.

"It is true, oysters in water columns grow faster than on bottom where they grow in the wild," allowed DNR's Judy. "To the degree oysters grow faster and escape disease, water column aquaculture can be helpful," he said. "But I won't say it's the savior of the oyster industry."

Breeding for Pearls

When you're talking pearls, you need more than a good bed. You've got to have good breeding.

"There's 40 years of selective breeding behind Circle C Lineback oyster," said Flynn, who came to Circle C as an intern from nearby St. Mary's College.

To perfect its strain of the Chesapeake Bay's native Eastern oyster, Circle C cultivates pedigreed oysters from genetic lines selected for growth rate, disease resistance, cup shape and thin shell. The deep cup and extra thin shell means a higher meat-to-shell ratio.

"Our oysters average about 32 percent more meat than the same size wild oyster," Flynn boasted.

Pelz and Flynn didn't get such a fine oyster all on their own. The Circle C Lineback is bred from the Chesapeake Supreme, a strain of Eastern oyster developed by Frank 'Buddy' Wilde, who traces his roots back four generations on the Shady Side peninsula.

A pioneer aquaculturist of an earlier age, Wilde perfected his oyster back in the 1960s.

"Larvae is gregarious," Wilde told Bay Weekly. "It needs to be together. But when larvae gets together on a clump of shell, it doesn't give you a very good oyster."

His contribution was developing a way to get larvae to set one by one. When his oysters had grown to seed size, about as big as a quarter, he transferred them to floats: "simple trays six square feet that were easy to handle and that would hold a bushel of market size oysters."

His little hatchery in his Bayfront yard at Felicity Cove was a wooden structure 14 by 16 feet that looked "more like a farm tool shack." There, he produced more seed oysters than he could ever sell, so he sold to other growers.

Wilde also marketed Chesapeake Supremes himself, selling them to the seafood markets at Annapolis City Dock, to some local restaurants and to neighborhood customers in Shady Side. "Now they had the flavor," he said.

Wilde closed down his hatchery many years ago, so Circle C has to breed its oysters as well as farm them.

DNR runs hatcheries at Piney Point in St. Mary's County and Deal Island on the Eastern Shore; University of Maryland's Center for Environmental Science runs another hatchery on Horn Point in Cambridge. But Maryland's three state-owned hatcheries can't sell to commercial operations. The only private hatchery in the Bay is Middle Peninsula Aquaculture in Virginia. So to get their eggs, Circle C selects 60 or 70 of its best brood stock—"the largest, best cup-shaped oyster to form better meat," Flynn said—and sends them off to Virginia's Middle Peninsula.

By heating the water in its tanks, the hatchery provokes the oysters to spawn, producing eggs and sperm that quickly develop into larvae. The larvae swim free for about three weeks before they are shipped back to Circle C as transparent "eyed larvae" already forming miniature shells. The first shipments of six to seven million larvae arrive around the first of July.

"Ten million larva can fit in your hand," said Flynn, opening his own ample fist to show that the larvae shipments arriving by UPS from Middle Peninsula Aquaculture are smaller than a golf ball once they're unpacked.

On the Farm

On the Circle C dock on St. Jerome Creek, each crop begins with millions of well-bred larvae.

"Twenty percent is a good transition figure from larvae to seed oysters," said Pelz, explaining that by planting time, he's down to some 400,000 seed oysters.

Outfitted in apron and big rubber gloves, Pelz works over waist-high tanks, called downwellers and upwellers, to nurture oyster seed through the delicate nursery stage.

The tiny larvae's first stop is the downweller. Take away the fancy name and you get an open plastic bucket, the sort that holds drywall compound, with fine mesh screening stretched across the top. Just as low-tech is the fine layer of crushed oyster shell that is the larvae's first bed. Pelz pulverizes the shell in his electric coffee grinder.

On the screen, larvae are poured onto shell, and creek water is piped through the downweller. At that stage, Pelz explained, "three larvae can swim side by side through one hole in a window screen."

Many screen-sized changes later, the inch-long survivors are moved into roomy mesh bags, where they grow to market size in Pelz's floating reefs. Eighteen or so months from set, some 125,000 oysters are harvested.

From Farm to Market

On the farm, oysters are harvested year round, but demand is greatest in winter. Most days this season, Circle C brings in its harvest.

Pelz and Flynn raise the floating reefs with a pulley, cut open the mesh bags and grade their crop. Oysters are separated into three sizes: cocktail, two and a half to three inches; standard, three to three and a half inches; and large, four and over.

Drive down Route 235 in St. Mary's County to Airdale Road, and you can buy Circle Cs on the dock where they grew, for $6 a dozen. Shop at Woodburn's Market in Solomons, and you'll pay $10 a dozen for Circle Cs. Order Circle Cs on the half shell at McCormick & Schmick—an upscale West Coast seafood restaurant with a Bethesda location—and you'll pay far more. Circle Cs are on the menu there and at a dozen more fancy restaurants, from Leonardtown to D.C.

Other Circle C customers are environmentalists and entrepreneurs who want to grow their own oysters. To encourage oyster-culture, the Maryland General Assembly last year passed legislation—sponsored by delegates George Owings, from Southern Maryland, and John Hurson—granting an income tax credit for 100 percent of the purchase price of aquaculture oyster floats for personal, non-commercial use, up to a maximum credit of $500.

"We sold over 100 floats since the legislation, as opposed to 13 last year," Pelz said.

Commercial oyster ranchers are buying floats, too, as well as oysters to stock them. Two St. Mary's County ranchers each have 80 to 100 floats in the water. When their oysters reach market size—an average four to six inches—in six months, they sell them back to Circle C as a cash crop.

Saving the Bay

As proof of his claim to grow oysters faster than disease can kill them, Pelz harvested 125,000 oysters this season.

But he can do more. Pelz said he can indeed save the Bay by saving its native oyster.

The secret, he said, is his floating reef, under patent as the Biological Nutrient Control System.

To understand how salvation might work, you have to imagine how bivalves and Bay work together: When the Bay was healthy, so were oysters, for each satisfied the other's needs. The Bay brought the oysters sunlight and nutrients; the oysters filtered the Bay, keeping it clean. Only when human acts broke that system down did disease run wild.

Put enough oysters back in the Bay, Pelz said, and the balance will be restored. As farmed oysters grow, they'll filter the water from the top down, stimulating photosynthesis and creating oxygen to restore the symbiosis of bivalve and Bay.

"The native oysters grow fine, they just need a chance," said Pelz.

He said each three-inch oyster filters 50 gallons of water a day, so each of Circle C's five-bag rafts contain about a thousand oysters, which filter about 50,000 gallons of water a day. Multiply that action by each new reef planted by oyster entrepreneurs, and everybody would be happy. The Bay would be clean. Oysters would be fat. So would oyster farmers, if Pelz's estimate that one-tenth of an acre farmed actively could yield an annual $50,000 crop of oysters.

That's why Richard Pelz thinks his "market-based solution to pollution control" is a pearl of an idea.

Let's hope he's right.

—January 9, 2003

UPDATE: 2021

Richard Pelz's pearl of an idea proved bright enough to survive the vicissitudes of the first two decades of the 21st century, including recession, Covid-19 and Lyme disease. Circle C Oyster Ranch still farms oysters on St. Jerome Creek.

"I was crippled up with Lyme, but I got over it," Pelz reported in mid-January 2021. "These days, I'm feeling very young."

That good news has to do not only with recovery but also with love.

"I'm engaged to a sweet girl in the Philippines. I'm going to get her this week, and she's going to come back with me and work with me at Circle C Oyster Ranch," Pelz said in a telephone interview.

He expects that partnership to reinvigorate the business, which retrenched in recent years. Table oysters, sold retail off his dock, are now only a small part of his business. More of his oysters have a precautionary mission.

He sells seed oysters about an inch long to "laboratories to test new chemicals coming onto the market." Larger oysters take the role of canaries in a coal mine, acting as monitors to "pick up potential leaks in the discharge water" at Calvert Cliffs Nuclear Power Plant.

As the story you've just read suggests, oysters are versatile creatures.

Sandra Olivetti Martin

New Bay Books publisher

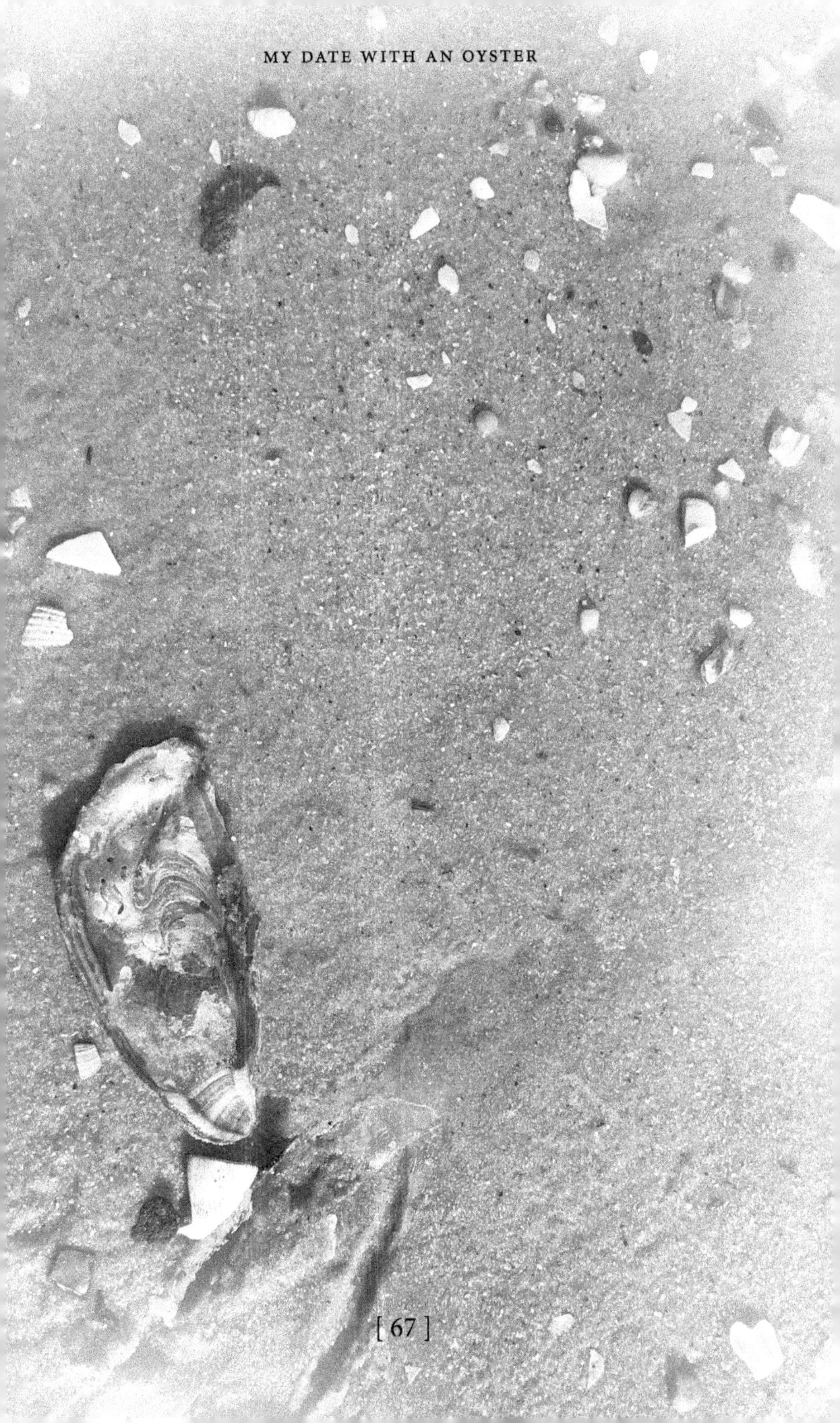

- three -

Seasonal Reflections

April - May

April
Earth Journal
Spring Fever Is Just Another Name for Spring Cleaning

In spring, there's an energy that just won't quit. What's infectious in nature spreads to humans with no harm done. Catching this fever just means getting caught up on some long overdue chores.

It's easy to get caught up in the activity in Bay country.

Tundra swans are heeding the call of nesting grounds up north. Many have already gone. Preparing for their flight, morning, noon and into sunset they are on training missions of military force, if not always precision. Each day they fly to higher altitudes, alter the size of their vee and scatter, only to converge again from all directions. Is organized disorganization their strategy, as it is ours sometimes?

How to get everyone in sync after a winter of taking it easy is an annual challenge. To this seasonal test, there are as many approaches as there are species.

For several years running, a pair of bluebirds has shown up in my yard right around the time the swans depart. I'm not sure why these industrious little creatures were paired with the noun happiness. They may be cheerful, but the bluebirds I've seen are far too serious to be particularly pleased. From the moment they hit the yard they are all action, all business. There's not a moment to lose, or so it seems.

Decisions weigh heavy: choose the box near the willow and birch trees or the one near the rose bush but closer to the driveway. Or how about that other nice yard? All the while the male is coaxing the female—or is it the other way around?

If bluebirds could frown, spring would be the time. So many choices, so little time. Sound familiar?

Nature's nest builders taunt us with their exuberance. Sweeping out the old, piling on the new. With all this high energy in the air, maybe it's time to get our own brood in gear. Most families in my neighborhood would rather keep their heads in the clouds, like the swans. But we are earthbound, and spring chores call. A vernal deadline is still a deadline.

Less sublime and at ground level, the garden needs clearing, the garage is brimful, and houses wait, inside and out, for a fresh coat of paint. Lawn equipment needs checking. Pruning time is here. It's not too early to plant a garden and look, someone's already cutting their grass!

How all this energy is contagious, just when we're feeling the first signs of spring fever, is a wonder. Maybe that's the joke played on us right around the first of April. We're down with a contagious fever, but no harm is done.

We can't quit now: How would it look to the bluebirds of busyness in the backyard?

—April 2, 1997

Walkers make their way across the Chesapeake Bay Bridge. *Photo by Kathleen Wilson.*

Reflection

Feet, Don't Fail Me as I Walk Across the Bay

Crab pots pepper the water far below and the big blue sky seems close enough to touch when you're striding over the big Bay Bridge.

Of course every journey begins with a single step. On this journey, you take that step at the Navy-Marine Corps Stadium in Annapolis, where walkers stand in a serpentine line that adds a not-inconsiderable distance to the 4.3-mile length of the span across the Chesapeake Bay.

From the stadium, you'll eventually be ferried to the bridge and across to the Eastern Shore starting point by buses flashing digital messages: *Maryland You Are Beautiful and Bridge Walk.* But it can take a couple of hours before you climb aboard. First, you've got a long, slow serpentine warm-up in the huge parking lot.

"If you have the patience to go through this," said '99 walker Charles Jackson of Temple Hills, "you can enjoy the walk." As he has every Bridge Walk since 1982, when, Jackson said, the Blue Angels entertained.

The seemingly endless line makes for plenty of quality time getting to know your neighbors. New-found friends exchange notes on children, the cost of education, investments, personal philosophies, places to go, even medical treatments. Many pick up tips for next year's walk, like bringing a flag so members of their group can find their way back in line when they return from standing in another line—for Porta Potties.

Why are you walking? everybody wants to know. It's the second most popular question, following *have you walked before?*

Jackson's walking partner, Theresa Blackburn of Mitchellville—a fifth-timer dressed in a crisp, emerald green wind suit—gave her reason as "something to do." Both also "do it for the exercise."

1999 walkers Dennis and Mary Rose Grinestaff of Baltimore "wanted to do the walk for years, but something always came up." This was their year, though they'd only learned last year's walk date at a shrimp feast the night before and were walking on "only a few hours sleep."

When you finally get on the bus, you're in for a treat. Crossing to the Eastern Shore to begin your walk, the view from the bus of thousands of walkers is a marvel. Your excitement is fueled by knowing that soon, you, too, will be out there, walking high over the Bay.

But even when you get to the other side, you'll have to run a gauntlet of vendors selling hot dogs, crab cakes and funnel cakes.

Finally, the real Bay Bridge Walk begins. Babies and grandparents, teenagers and toddlers join moms and dads in a high-minded sea of humanity rolling along the bridge deck, 186 feet above the Chesapeake Bay. Pods of fishing boats and sailboats bob in the water below. A gunshot piercing this peaceful all-Maryland Sunday is only the start of a sailboat race below.

Dressed in tank tops and Polartec, earmuffs and sandals, pushing strollers or pulling red Radio Flyer wagons piled with kids, the sea of walkers rolls on. Some roll along to the finish line with the help of canes and wheelchairs. All wear smiles a mile wide—though they might be thinking *feet—bridge—don't fail me now.* All walk away with a certificate signed by Gov. Parris Glendening.

Then it's back in line for the buses back to the stadium. But the line moves swiftly, thanks to efficient MTA bus drivers who have also had a long day.

May
Earth Journal
Welcome as the Flowers

My father had an expression. "You're as welcome as the flowers in May," he'd tell friends and guests to our home. The phrase sounds quaint and old fashioned now, but the truth is, the man who had never known a stranger also loved flowers, especially roses, as much as he did people.

Every spring, Dad predicted his roses would bloom by Mother's Day. So May is when I expect my roses to bloom.

The author's father: John Patrick Faunce. *Faunce family photo.*

Growing roses is tricky business. I can remember when I got disillusioned about life. It wasn't dirty politics or a relationship gone sour. It was when I found out that other parts of the country aren't pestered by Japanese beetles. Pop's roses had those pesky insects, too, but as a kid they seemed more like iridescent ornaments than the weapons of destruction they are to me now. I don't remember his roses having black spot or aphids, though perhaps they did. He never used a chemical or took a Master Gardener's class. He just watered and pruned his roses sharply about the time the forsythia bloomed.

The man loved roses. When my mother and sister and I went off to a party or school or work, to the cemetery or on a social call, my Dad would hand us a bouquet of cut roses to take along. Spring through fall, there was always a pot of freshly cut roses on the table and in the windowsill. I can still picture the table set on my May birthday with a vase of fragrant hybrid tea and old-fashioned roses sitting next to my cake.

So in May, I expect the roses in my yard to bloom. But in my day, the simple act of growing roses has gotten complicated. Roses are said to need about six hours of full sun, good air circulation and a soil PH of 6.5, a little on the acid side. Dad's roses grew under a shady canopy of huge spreading elms. He never counted the canes when he pruned, and he never fertilized or used a fungicide. I doubt his soil was a perfect 1-1-1 mix of the clay, organic matter and sand roses are said to prefer. I never once saw him mulch the top of the plant's bud union for protection (though he often sipped a cold Bud as he admired his healthy blooms). And forget it: Spraying his plants with horticultural or dormant oil would have been out of the question for this natural gardener.

As Mother's Day approaches, I'm getting nervous about the roses in my Bay Country garden. I can't be sure there will be flowers to cut for the cemetery or my birthday table. But I do know this. If I take a walk down East Capitol Street in Washington, D.C., where I grew up as a kid, there will be roses blooming. They were planted by a man who never knew a stranger and who loved a rose.

Reflection

Message to My Mother

This is not a political commentary, but around this time in the month of May, I'm reminded of the best comment I ever knew Ronald Reagan to make, certainly the truest. "We're never prepared to lose our mothers," he once wrote to a friend and White House associate whose mother had just died.

The president offered comfort by expressing something all of us know intuitively, but have a hard time defining—that we are connected to our mothers by a bond that is both permanent and intangible.

When I was in school, a nun put it this way: the father is the head of the home; the mother, its heart. While that view may be outdated in today's changing family, the significance of a mother's place in our lives is not. Whether we were raised by our birth mother or a caring surrogate, the ties that bind us are infinite—and infinitely complex.

Three Faunce women: little sister Mary Louise, big sister Joanne and mother, Florence. *Faunce family photo.*

For those of us whose mothers are no longer living, Mother's Day is sometimes bittersweet. The first Mother's Day after my own mother died was not as hard as the second, however.

That first year, I decided on the spur of the moment to fly to my sister's for a visit. What could be more comforting than to be in the company of this sweet woman? Ours is a relationship defined by the ease of finishing each other's sentences in those moments when needed most.

How could I be anything but cheered in the company of her three children, who had had such a special connection with their grandmother? Earlier that year, the youngest granddaughter had read to her Nana at bedside at Hospice. The strength of someone so very young and the patience of one so near God's door were extraordinary. A little girl who once described her grandmother as "soft and pink" also learned the meaning of courage.

The second Mother's Day, spent at home, was harder. That Sunday seemed a little like being in a foreign country on a national holiday and not being part of the celebration. We don't separate ourselves from situations so much as we sometimes just move to another seat for a while where everything looks different.

A radio program called Stained Glass Bluegrass offered unexpected comfort. We take solace whenever any expression seems genuine, as these songs did. If you haven't heard Hank Williams Sr. sing "Message to my Mother," you're in for a soothing surprise.

The Mother's Days that followed, including this one, are spent like everyone else's: enjoying a day that celebrates a concept that can't be cloned. "A mother's love" is not a cliché: It is the tender care given us so that we, too, may learn the value of nurturing our own young. On Mother's Day, in person, or in memory, we pay tribute to the one person in the whole world who loves us unconditionally—whether we realize it or not.

Mother's Day can put a song in your heart or a twang in your song, if you're a bluegrass fan. It is a very good day to say—aloud or in the quiet of our hearts—"I love you, Mom."

May 7, 1998

The Whole Crab—And Nothing But the Crab

In Maryland's Crab Picking Industry, Everything's Used, Nothing's Wasted

Marylanders love their crabs, but we've loved like Shakespeare's Othello, not wisely but too well. Mountains of shell discarded after a crab feast tell the story of us as consumers, our insatiable appetite for crabs, our habits of consumption and waste.

In Maryland's crab picking industry, it's a different story. There, everything's used, nothing's wasted. We followed the division of the whole crab into a product greater than the sum of its parts at the J.M. Clayton Company in Cambridge, which calls itself the "oldest working crab processing plant in the world."

Founded in 1890 by Captain Johnnie Clayton and today operated by great-grandsons Jack, Joe and Bill Brooks, J.M. Clayton Seafood Company is one of some 25 crab processing plants in 21st century Maryland, most on the Eastern Shore's Dorchester County. The number is down sharply from some 60 plants in the 1980s and many more in earlier years. Maryland seafood processing plants may be a fading industry, but not because of any deficit on the part of owners and employees. The packing-house floor is a whirlwind of energy, vitality and sheer determination.

From Live to Steamed

Within the hour after Atlantic blue crabs arrive at the dock, their division into delicious and useful products begins.

Self-employed crab potters and trotliners off-load their booty of beautiful swimmers onto Clayton's prime Cambridge Choptank riverfront dock. There a Clayton worker culls and grades them, setting aside the best for the "table trade." Crabs at least five and three-quarters inches point to point are destined for restaurants, where they'll be steamed and devoured in copious quantity. Crabs with no "live trade" market—females and legal, smaller male crabs—get cooked.

From bushel baskets (imported, incidentally from Little Rock, Arkansas) stacked on the dock, it's a short ride on a short pier, a momentary reprieve before crabs are emptied into steel baskets the size of an SUV. Clayton's two four-by-six-foot vats each hold 400 pounds of squirming, scrapping crabs. The fight soon will be steamed out of them as they're plunged into 250-degree steam for seven minutes.

At Clayton's on a mid-summer's day, 350 bushels of crabs will be so handled. In late summer and fall, when many say crabs are at their fattest and the table trade slackens, a staggering 1,000 bushels of crabs a day are processed at the Choptank River plant.

Pickers work by hand, with knives,
filling plastic containers with short use-by-date deadline and
cans to be pasturised by long use-by date. *Photo by M.L. Faunce.*

Hand Picking

Crabs are in good supply this time of year—for this year at least—and a bumper crop reaches the docks. It's the pickers who are in short supply, as Marylanders forsake a trade that's seasonal, monotonous and painstaking. Emergency legislation sponsored by Sen. Barbara Mikulski saved the day for Maryland crab processing plants, and Congress approved her bill allowing temporary visas for guest workers from Mexico to fill empty crab-picking and -packing jobs.

With guest visa issues resolved for this year and next, all hands are at work. Crab picking is a trade ruled by women; traditionally, men crack only the claws. The women's hands are swift and sure, moving seamlessly as if their fingers flow into the action of their knives. Their minds and bodies seem detached, so concentrated is the automation. They move quicker than the eye, slicing off the crabs' swimming legs, cross-sectioning and dissecting the body. Most work barehanded, but some wear a single rubber glove.

At Clayton, pickers must produce a minimum of 18 pounds of crabmeat a day. Crab pickers are paid $2.25 per pound of meat picked. They get no benefits.

Experience counts when it comes to picking, and the best, like 53-year-old Georgia 'Sissy' Cephas, a picker for 25 years, can race the clock through a bushel of crabs piled high in front of her. Each day, she picks "30, 40 even 50 pounds," said Jack Brooks.

Sissy and each of her sister-pickers develop their own style of picking. Speed as well as style follow experience.

Clayton's Epicure pound containers lined before the pickers tell the hierarchy of crabmeat. From top to bottom, it's jumbo lump, lump, special and claw, and each crab contributes some to each pot.

Each picker is assigned a number that's marked on each bottom of the container she picks. That's how her pay is counted, and if you find too much shell, you can complain that number so and so did not carefully add only crab and no shell to her product.

By house rules, pickers break each hour and a half. They stretch their backs and fingers, then carry their cans and plastic cups of crabmeat across the packinghouse to the inspection station. At each mandatory break, pickers wash their hands and sanitize their trays and knives.

53-year-old Georgia 'Sissy' Cephas, has picked crabs at the J.M. Clayton Company in Cambridge for 25 years. *Photo by M.L. Faunce.*

There fourth-generation Clayton scion Clay Brooks, Jack's son, oversees quality-control inspectors Leona Travers and Shelly Neal. The packed cans are weighed, and crab is added or removed to make each a true pound.

Next the containers are sealed. A plastic lid is clapped on plastic tubs of fresh crabmeat meant to be eaten within days.

Metal cans of crabmeat will be, as the can reads, "pasteurized to retain its quality." But first they're lidded, one by one, in an ancient press at a top speed of 30 to 40 a minute, depending on the speed of the person pressing the lever. Canned crabmeat will then be pasteurized by cooking at 190 degrees for two hours. Stored at 38 degrees—not frozen—as the can advises, it's good for six months to a year. Joe Brooks says he's sampled pasteurized crabmeat canned and refrigerated years ago; it was still good. He prefers pasteurized. "It's always as fresh as the day it was caught."

Finally the sealed containers are packed in layers of ice inside a cardboard box for shipping. They'll be trucked tonight and delivered tomorrow in Baltimore, Washington and southern Pennsylvania, where one of Claytons' big customers is Giant Foods, Pennsylvania.

It's true handwork every step of the way, and all done basically the same way since 1890. Today, though, Brooks says the company complies with rules set by 23 separate regulatory agencies.

Nowadays, Maryland crabmeat is a high-end product, and hand-picking adds to the gourmet label and the price tag. Its taste is described as sweet, and, yes, it's possible to taste the difference.

"Imported *Portunus pelagicus* crab is a little larger on average than our *Callinectes sapdius* and has a much deeper body, allowing a larger lump and less shell," explained Noreen Eberly, Maryland's director of seafood marketing. "The crab meat is very white, due to processing and the addition of sodium acid pyrophosphate. Our crabmeat is more of a cream color that includes the flavorful fat and no additives or preservatives.

"Each day," says co-owner Jack Brooks, above,
"she picks 30, 40 even 50 pounds." *Photo by M.L. Faunce.*

"Side by side, the imported looks prettier," Eberly said, "but Maryland crab meat tastes better. We have done consumer taste-test panels in Maryland, Virginia and North Carolina that testify to that."

Even so, to keep up with price competition and to counter declining native supplies, even Brooks is considering supplementing Clayton's Maryland Epicure brand with imported crab. "I see a need and probably should have earlier, so I don't want to ignore the possibility," said Joe Brooks. "But the Bay is still good to us."

Can a Machine Pick Crab?

As the picking and packing houses ramp up for the October and November deluge of crabs, even the 50 pickers at Clayton's aren't enough to keep up. When crabs outnumber pickers, the slack is taken up by a picking machine developed in the 1970s when the industry first felt labor shortages.

The efficient machine can top even the best hand-picker, unshelling 180 crabs a minute for 2,200 pounds—that's 400 to 500 bushels—a day. The mechanized process carries crabs by a system of conveyor belts. First, trays of cooked crab are softened on a steam table leading to an airbag-like mechanism that shakes the crabs violently for a second or two, releasing meat from shell. The meat is deposited onto a belt and inspected for shell by human eyes.

So a machine can pick crab. But even the best machine can't preserve the lovely great chunks that make lump crab meat—a 50-50 combination of special and lump—worth $18 a pound and jumbo lump—$23 at Clayton's plant. A crab-picking machine breaks up the lumps when it shakes out the meat, which is sold as flake meat under the special label for $13 a pound.

A good hand-picker can crack 30 pounds of the fattest, meatiest claws a day into cocktail fingers, sold on site for $10 a pound. That's seven bushels, according to Joe Brooks. These whole cracked crab claws line a can as pretty as might a gardener's put-up jars of string beans, circling the container in precise rounded rows.

Joe Brooks, above, operates with his brothers the J.M. Clayton Company, founded in 1890 by his great-grandfather Capt. Johnnie Clayton. *Photo by M.L. Faunce.*

But there's no way even the best pickers can keep up with all the claws. So at this time of year the Harris machine goes to work.

Whole claws are fed through a reel that washes them into a hammer mill, where they're broken up. Next, the salinity in a salt-water bath makes the meat float and the shell sink. The meat overflows onto a perforated belt, where it's rinsed with fresh water, inspected for shell then drained and packed. Machine picked claw meat sells for $10 a pound on site.

Waste Not, Want Not

There's more shell than meat in any crab, and all those thousands of pounds of crab leave potentially huge waste piles. But in this business, nothing goes to waste.

Crabs have eight swimming legs, about which Brooks said, "you can't make a meal from them, but they contain a lot of meat, protein and flavor. Another machine goes to work making mincemeat of those legs, the picked-over shells the back shell and the fat. Baader meat, so named for the German-invented machine that extracts remainder meat for a flavoring paste, is sold in five-pound packs to processors and restaurants for soups and filler for crab products and seasoning.

Even the shell, the garbage of home and restaurant crab feasts, is not wasted at Maryland crab-picking plants. The last of the crab, the Baader machine

All the crab pickers are women, and much of the seasonal labor force comes from Mexico. *Photo by M.L. Faunce.*

waste, is trucked to New Earth Services in the Dorchester County town of Hurlock.

There it's processed into Chesapeake Blue, weed-free compost for lawns, vegetable gardens, flowerbeds, shrubs and tress, fall-planted bulbs and potted plants.

"Crab shells are rich in nitrogen, but they need the addition of sawdust to balance carbon and nitrogen," explained Pat Condon, president of the 12-year-old Earth Services. "When the two are combined, micro-organisms thrive. Temperatures reach 160 degrees, and all the bad bacteria are killed. Six or eight months down the road, we've got an odor-free, shelf-stable compost."

New Earth Services produces 1,000 tons of Chesapeake Blue a year from 1,000 tons of crab shell and 1,000 tons of sawdust.

Loved well and sometimes wisely, blue crabs give us their all.

—September 29, 2005

UPDATE: 2021

J.M. Clayton Seafood Company continues to buy, steam, pick and market crab. The business is nowadays a rarity, one of under 20 to survive the stressed economy with fewer crabs and fewer pickers. In 2021, a great-great grandson from the fifth generation has joined the business.

In 2020, in prime season between 250 and 350 bushels of crab a day were processed with the labor of 80 some pickers, including women who travel annually from Mexico under scarce H2-B visas.

Chesapeake Blue is no longer in business to compost all that shell and waste; it is now sold to farmers for agricultural fertilizer.

Clayton deals only in Atlantic blue crab, but the once-ubiquitous Chesapeake crab remains too scarce to supply the demand of J.M. Clayton or of Maryland's crab eaters—certainly not the Eastern seaboard.

Were there not so many eaters, crab numbers would seem astronomical. Four hundred and five million crabs prowled the Chesapeake in 2020, a near-average abundance over 30 years. The region-wide harvest last year was almost sixty-one million pounds, with Maryland's share thirty-three million pounds. The dockside value of Maryland crab was $47 million in 2017.

But with crab on every seafood house menu, Maryland picking houses buy their blue crab from wherever they can get it, down the Atlantic coast and into the Gulf. Imported Asian species flood commercial markets, so you never know if you're buying Atlantic blue crab unless you ask. Or unless you buy J.M. Clayton Seafood Company's Epicure brand. It's highest grade, jumbo lump, sells at the Cambridge, Maryland plant for $40 a pound.

Maryland crab continues to be a delicacy for all who do not catch their own.

Sandra Olivetti Martin
New Bay Books publisher

- four -

Seasonal Reflections

June - July

June
Earth Journal

Some Sounds of Summer Are Mostly Remembered

Just as much as crabbing, swimming, boating and visiting relatives on the South and Patuxent Rivers were part of my summers growing up, so was hearing the call of the bobwhite on still, steamy summer afternoons.

Now it seems I have to travel all the way down to my sister's home in southern Alabama to hear that singular call.

In the rural south, quail still thrive in a countryside of cotton and peanut fields, bordered by stands of long leaf pine and fragrant mimosa.

Here in Maryland, as agricultural lands shrink and development encroaches, some sounds of summer, like the bobwhite, are mostly remembered.

I haven't always heeded life's calls that sometimes beckon me from a state as lazy as a child's summer nap. But somehow, involuntarily, I've always returned the sweet summons of the bobwhite quail each time it calls. I did so again as it echoed across peaceful Alabama fields near my sister's home. But beauty is always easier to follow than duty, I suppose.

The truth is, I've never actually seen this small, plump bird the size of a robin. But I sure remember the pure sound of its whistle piercing the air like a cracking whip. Seeing this small game bird is a challenge anyway, with its mottled brown plumage that makes for effective camouflage. And of course seeing is not always believing; it's that distinctive call that's engrained in our senses that we recognize.

Living by the Bay for seven years now, I've heard the bobwhite but one season. DNR's bird expert Glenn Therres told me why. "Bobwhite are resident birds. They don't migrate," he said. "They either prosper or decline."

In Maryland, they are declining.

Though Therres lacks the exact figures he has for our expanding eagle population, he has the reason. "Bobwhite are birds of the field; their habitat is the forest edge, associated with agricultural lands," Therres explained.

In the past, some fields were left fallow, inviting nesting in the grasses between field and forest. Goldenrod and broom sedge added to the light cover bobwhite prefer. Now, most agricultural lands—and those are fewer each year—are actively farmed. To help, DNR pushes growing warm-season prairie grass-like crops to give the quail cover for nesting opportunity.

Inhabiting the "edge" between field and forest (and us), bobwhites are truly on the edge of life, with one of the highest rates of decline among birds. Therres describes the bobwhite as "pretty vocal with a sound that travels far over field and water." Perhaps the word hasn't traveled far enough, so that we are in danger of losing the uncommon call of this bird of field and summers past.

—June 18, 1997

Reflection

The Babe and the Boys: A Father's Day Memory

It's 10am at Lexington Market, in Baltimore, when I order a regular crabcake at the John W. Faidley seafood counter.

"The lump is better," I'm told, but I stick with the regular, a cake made from "special" grade crabmeat. Served on saltine crackers, it's deep fried and hot when I take my plate to a standup table to devour the delectable taste of the Bay.

On a hot, summer morning in Baltimore, so much can satisfy the soul, stir the memory.

I've come to Baltimore for more than summer pleasures. I've come to trace some family history recalling another summer day, now some three-quarters of a century ago. Then, on a warm afternoon in August of 1922, my dad's stepmother took him and his younger brothers, Henry and George, for a trip to the beach. Or at least that's what she told them as they pulled away from their home on N Street in Georgetown in Washington, D.C.

Their stepmother, Thelma, was an eccentric artist with slight interest in the ways and wonders of three young boys who had lost their own mother in the Spanish Flu epidemic. Instead of sand and sun and water, the boys found themselves at the doorstep of St. Mary's Industrial School, as far away as lads could be from a mother's love. When the gates clanked shut behind them, the imposing building ahead, it was a summer day they would not soon forget.

But some of the details would be forgotten over the years. Recently, my Uncle George, the only brother still living (he was six at the time) recalled that they went by streetcar and not automobile. "The old lady put us on board herself," according to his memory.

But what the brothers all remembered with clarity was the effect Babe Ruth had on their lives at St. Mary's. George Herman Ruth, a Baltimore waif but not an orphan, had preceded them at St. Mary's. From the time he was seven until he turned 19, from 1902 until 1914, and before he was called 'the Babe,' Ruth lived at the school. The Jesuits running the school became his family, his fathers, and St. Mary's the place he called home.

After Ruth left St. Mary's, he returned often to see 'the boys.' By then, they were his family, too. My dad recalled visits by the man who was a gentle giant around kids who were a lot like him, all members of a special club none had sought to join. "He'd reach in his pocket and press quarters in our hands," my dad once told me. "It made us feel like a million bucks."

Over the years, I've searched for clues to my dad's life, on summer days through the streets of Georgetown and Baltimore, not because this history was unknown to me, but to keep a connection that is forever a strength, constantly a gift.

Sometimes bits and pieces of my father's life come back in unexpected ways. Like finding my dad's grandfather's grave and pausing while the clerk read from a yellowing page now almost a century old.

"Buried extra deep. Refused to pay balance," the record read.

Apparently, my dad's stepmother, Thelma had gotten into a quarrel with the cemetery. Expecting to be charged for the long-overdue balance, inexplicably I began telling the story of my dad and his brothers and St. Mary's. I probably even mentioned 'the Babe.' A kindly face studied me carefully, then asked, "how did they turn out?"

"My dad and his brothers? Fine," I replied. "Just fine."

As I ended my summer day in Baltimore, I thought about the brothers who turned out to be loving fathers, family men to the hilt. Big men with big hearts and gentle ways, all. And I thought about 'the Babe,' who had made them feel like a million bucks for just a quarter.

—June 17, 1999

July
Earth Journal

Nourished by Rain

In Bay Country, fish swim, ponds brim. The Chesapeake is awash with fresh water, fed by daily rains, nearly absent of sea nettles. Our green summer world is wet and wild. At my yard, trees ever expanding in girth and leaf, march toward my deck, like an advancing army.

A niece visiting from out west luxuriates in the moisture of this verdant scene. A Marylander by birth, she misses the passing of the seasons, she says. Now she lives with wildfires the worst in five decades. Oh, for a rainy day, she sighs, and gets several while home.

For us, drought is over. Nothing is forever, of course. Still, we relish all that is nourished from this flourishing world that is ours this summer. All in nature prospers in the abundance. A frolicking foal seems to revel in the lush landscape. He nuzzles a fence near Crandell Road in Southern Anne Arundel County and grows as fast as the weeds in the field.

Corn sweetens, born of fertile loam and Mother Nature's kindness. Crape myrtle, weighted with magenta flowers, split and spill under heavy rains in Bayside front yards. Kudzu clutches all it can. Queen Anne's lace sprouts willy nilly. Sunflowers face east, their surest source of sun nurture. Bluebirds return to produce yet another brood in my yard. Black-eyed Susans wink, blink and nod. Tobacco flowers. A llama on Riva Road soaks its feet in a pond made for ducks, now drying out on the shore.

Cucumbers swell and keep their cool. Pick early and often. Fried green tomatoes reign when the red won't come. Kids will be playing football by the time these luscious fruit ripen. Only grape tomatoes give forth a blazing red sweetness.

My old dog no longer shivers in summer storms. Maybe she senses they'll be with us for a while. I take her behavior as a lesson that humans can get used to things, too. Like green tomatoes. Crickets and crabgrass and ground ivy. And a wet and wild summer that gives us all we want and more.

—August 24, 2000

Reflection

Summer, in Three Parts

You Live Someplace Long Enough,
You Are This Place.
—Rocky Balboa (Sylvester Stallone);
from the 2006 Rocky Balboa

The prescient words of Rocky Balboa, heavyweight champion of the movie screen, ring true for many of us.

Summer is a journey. It begins in June, ebbing and flowing like the tide. The Fourth of July intrudes and divides, confusing our summer senses. A glass half full or half empty? Just look at the newspaper with sales at Sears and K-Mart before we even get the hammock out.

This summer I went back to Alaska, a place I haven't lived in 20 years. Every time I visit, the mixed mantle of mountains and memories messes with my head—in a good way. Sliding seamlessly into June's endless northern daylight, truth is all around, all is transparent. The past and the future seem as clear as a bell. Maybe it's the air or the elevation.

On returning to the land of the last frontier, nothing seems to have changed. It's still a vast place, peopled with friendly folks, rivers full of big fish, mountains to climb, vistas galore up ahead. I mourn the changes man has wrought, but I revel in going back. I am this place.

In the East, in high-summer season, the seaboard beckons. Think down y'ocean. Maybe Jersey Shore. The Outer (or Inner) Banks. You know the feeling: gliding into the newness of June's longest days, slipping into your swimsuit, packing a picnic basket for your family just like ones your own mother packed. In summer, the past and the present intertwine. This scent of that cottage, the comfort of (and time for) a nap, this favorite fishing hole, that shady spot, a backyard picnic, a secret gunk hole. You are these places.

Fearful that summer will slip away, the tug for me is the state of Maine. The loon calls. So do lobster, and starry, two-blanket nights, cirrus clouds on high promising and delivering fair weather, and water so clean a baby could drink, though it's tasted mostly by dogs lying hard by the dock, rousing from their temporary lair close enough to shore to slurp at will. This place I have only lived in summer, but I am this place, too.

One thing I know: She who goes up in summer must come down. EZ Pass smoothes the way now, though for me without the happy racket of past summers. Dogs now long gone would jump and howl at toll booths en route. EZ Pass is a quiet ride, sometimes too quiet, if you know what I mean. I miss the friendly smiles of surprised toll takers in the clamor of passing.

Coming home to Bay Country in August, I find tomatoes full and red, ripened on the vine. Corn and melons still plentiful and sweet are peddled from roadside stands. Crabs have grown fat; my neighbor Jim can attest to that from his regular West River weekend haul. Osprey now have other fish to fry: nesting season behind, a journey ahead. The sounds of frogs and birds that filled the air night and day defining early summer give way to the steady chirp of crickets. That, too, will cease as nights cool.

The rhythms of summer may change, but they stay with us, waiting to emerge in another time and place.

On the cusp of change, at summer's end, we're reluctant to give up the flowers, though fruit will follow as reward. School's early start pushes us forward, ready or not. Scattered rains are softening lawns brittle from summer heat, but the evening air is thick and moist and brackish—mixing memory with desire, as the poem goes. Oysters come to mind, though we shall have to wait another month or more.

You live some places long enough, you are those places.

Bald eagle.
Photo by Craig Koppie, U.S. Fish and Wildlife Service.

Eagles inhabit the heavenly heights
They know neither limit nor bound
They're guardian angels of darkness and light
They see all and hear every sound ...
—Eagles and Horses by John Denver

Close Encounters With Eagles

These Days, Ever Closer

If the pair of bald eagles trying out the tallest loblolly pine tree in my Churchton, Maryland neighborhood stays to set up housekeeping, our community might be on the verge of a name change.

Our small settlement was named for the tundra swans that migrate to the Chesapeake region each winter to feed. Separated from the Bay by a hundred yards or so of rich wetlands, The Swans are used to the company of wildlife: stately herons, marauding raccoons, lumbering turtles, raucous gulls, busy rabbits and a host of melodic song birds watched by keen-eyed hawks.

Just as the swans capture our attention each fall migration, these mature bald eagles have seized our imagination. Watching them has become the neighborhood pastime.

Eagles Encountered

They don't look like fair-weather birds. Yet it's most often been on clear, crisp mornings that over the years I would catch sight of a bald eagle. Occasionally, a pair perched in a snag of a tree on Rockhold Creek. We welcomed the big birds for many reasons. Bald eagles are truly American, unique to our continent alone.

But most of all, we hail the eagle because of the attention it commands. The American bald eagle is of formidable size and beauty: males weigh in at seven to 10 pounds; females reach upward to 14 pounds. The wingspan is so significant—six to eight feet for male and female—that it conveys a mythical image. At maturity, around four to five years old, come the distinctive features we all recognize: white head and upper body feathers, broad white tail.

Flying at great heights, the eagle sees—some say hears—all, as it scouts for prey and nesting spots. To see it best, mere humans use binoculars. Observing the intensity of an eagle's eyes under this close scrutiny, you begin to understand the magnitude and power of the bird. Peering through binoculars at startling pale eyes looking back at me in my own yard, I'm reminded of a trip I made a few years ago to a raptor rehab center in Sitka, Alaska. There, in the land of eagles, I saw birds that had suffered mishaps, perhaps tangling with a fishing net, being nursed back to health before release to the wild. Staff there had penned a caption to a particularly vivid photo of a rescued eagle. I am smiling, the bird in the photo insisted.

From this safe distance, this year I watch the passion and intensity of instinctive behavior.

Eagles Move In

Perched at the crook of a tall, top-heavy pine, with head and neck feathers ruffled ever so slightly, the eagle does seem to be smiling. But it's a startled, wary kind of smile that makes you think he knows the dangers of human interference. Even so, he has chosen our home for his. I am looking full into the face and eyes of the eagle sitting on a nest in the early stages of construction. Good day by good day, stick by stick the nest grows. Engineering takes time, and eagles sometimes build multiple nests.

Some days sticks rain down in my yard. Sticks 12 inches long, sticks four feet long, which the eagle harvests from carefully selected trees. The dead wood, snapped under the eagle's weight, is carried off in its thick talons to the nest. This nest-building activity is as basic as food: Both are the sustenance of life.

The eagles who see all and hear all began their occupation here by telling all. One morning a juvenile eagle—still mottled not yet having grown its distinctive markings—flew around the new nest in youthful exuberance. In their nest, sitting close together as if on a small throne, the pair squawked out a warning. Their high-pitched call sounded like a rusty gate closing: not a garden gate but a huge metallic stockyard gate, bumping and reverberating as it closed. Well warned, the juvenile retreated.

When and if completed, this nest will measure four to five feet across and rest only about 20 feet from the nearest house in this area of many houses, all keeping their close vigil on the eagles' progress.

Eagle Nest

"This is serious business," said Glenn Therres, Department of Natural Resources biologist and eagle expert.

"They're not just carrying sticks for the heck of it. There's only one purpose, and that's nesting." The next nearest eagles' nest is in West River, Therres said, with another pair farther south near the Calvert-Anne Arundel county line.

"We get excited," he added, "when we hear about eagles building nests."

Nests are Therres' business. From a small, fixed-wing plane, he conducts an annual March-through-May aerial survey of eagle nesting areas. The nests he's seeking, usually located in the uppermost crotch of the tree, are tabulated for the record. After flying to all known spots, Therres searches for new nests.

This time, he's flying over Churchton, too. Early in March, the Churchton couple began lining their nest with soft pine boughs they'd plucked from trees.

"If the eagles are putting in soft pine boughs," said Therres, "they're lining the nest. Basically then, they're done building and are getting ready to lay their eggs.

However, he added, "these might be young birds in their first year nesting and may be a little out of sync with typical habits." In other words, there's no telling what they're up to.

Fuzzy, four-week-old eaglets.
Photo by Craig Koppie, U.S. Fish and Wildlife Service.

Once eggs are laid, they are incubated in about 35 days. So we shall see.

Everyone has their binoculars trained on that tall loblolly pine, and the presence of the eagles seems to have us thinking about how we treat the habitat we now share as we wait for nature to take its course.

Whatever the outcome this year, we know there will be next year. In Bay Country we have all the breeding habitat eagles like: wetlands and open water and a great big sky to circle in the drafts of air.

We may not decide to change the name of our neighborhood from The Swans to Eagles Nest. But as the nesting instinct rises and spring tides ebb, we celebrate this major comeback of America's symbol of freedom, the bald eagle, right in our own backyard.

Closer Encounters

When Warren Heising of Churchton stepped out of his house one recent morning, his thoughts were focused about knee high—getting his two young children off to daycare. But when a large tree branch fell from the sky to the ground nearby, Heising caught a surprised glimpse of the culprit: a bald eagle soaring overhead. The eagle was carrying sticks to a nest it was building in a tree in the yard next to his.

Increasingly, Bay country is eagle country, and close encounters with our national bird are no longer uncommon. Dwellers along Bay, creeks and rivers are often entertained with the sight of eagles perching in tall trees or cruising the shoreline in their hunt for food.

"Chesapeake Bay eagles have a tolerance for people, maybe even more than other eagles," said Department of Natural Resources wildlife biologist Glenn Therres.

While wildlife enthusiasts and bird lovers couldn't be happier about sharing Chesapeake Country with eagles, the eagles may not have much of a choice. The steadily expanding population of eagles over the last 10 years may mean that optimal nesting sites are becoming more limited. In fact, habitat loss may be our eagles' biggest problem.

Today, the bald eagle is more threatened than endangered, thanks to the apostolate of Rachel Carson, whose poignant book, *Silent Spring*, alerted Americans to the devastating effects of pesticides like DDT, helping to bring about its ban in the 1970s.

Thirty years ago, only about 40 nesting pairs were known in Maryland. In 1997, 219 nesting pairs were

Eagle flies overhead.
Photo by Craig Koppie, U.S. Fish and Wildlife Service.

counted in our state, and they hatched more than 280 young. There are probably another 300 or 400 eagles not yet of breeding age. When eagles from northern states like Maine converge here in winter, the population can soar to 1,000 or 1,500.

CLOSE ...

Eagles have about reached their sustainable population in Chesapeake Country, according to Craig Koppie, a biologist with the U.S. Fish and Wildlife Service's Chesapeake Office in Annapolis. Koppie has probably had more up-close and personal experience with eagles than just about anyone else around, having climbed into over 60 nests to band four-month-old chicks during a 10-year study of eagles by the federal government to monitor nest productivity.

How does the fierce-looking raptor appear at the tender age of four weeks?

"Quite cute," Koppie reported. "The chicks have fluffy gray down, but they're all feet and head, and both look bigger than the body." But watch out: by eight or nine weeks, these eaglets are as large as adults.

"It has been extremely rewarding, both personally and professionally to watch the progress," said Koppie, who also takes a picture record of the eagles he works with. "When I started some 20 years ago, it was not a common thing to see eagles. Now crossing the Potomac between Maryland and Virginia, I can see an eagle a day," Still, the biologist said, "we're at a crossroads. The conflicts are frequent, contact is increasing, and so is development."

An adult bald eagle, still too young to have grown the telltale white head feathers. *Photo by Craig Koppie, U.S. Fish and Wildlife Service.*

Glenn Therres, DNR's eagle man, has also seen increasing conflicts. Monitoring and recording nesting sites by aerial survey, he sees how human terrain and eagle domain intermingle. To resolve conflict, he works with county and state planning jurisdictions, including developers. In areas not already zoned, DNR can help establish buffers to protect the eagles.

CLOSER ...

Last fall, an eagle encounter in Annapolis pointed out the unexpected challenges posed when wildlife and humans become close neighbors. Stephen Reed, a ranger at Quiet Waters Park, took an early morning phone call from neighbors living just outside the park in Bay Ridge. Kendel and Marta Taut had awakened that rainy Sunday morning in October to find two mature bald eagles down and distressed in their backyard.

"One bird's talons were sunk into the side of the other bird, and the talons would stay attached as long as the other bird kept pressure on or struggled," Reed said.

The birds, possibly fighting over food or territory, might have become attached in the air before falling into the Taut's backyard, Reed speculated. When he arrived on the scene, the eagles appeared to be suffering from exhaustion and shock.

They needed to be separated, quickly, but help wasn't quickly available.

Department of Natural Resources—where Reed was challenged as to whether he could tell eagles from osprey—had no wildlife officer on duty over the weekend. Noah's Ark, a wildlife shelter in Pasadena, was likewise short staffed.

Reed was advised to capture the eagle and bring it in. He called that bad advice. "I've had 30 years of experience and training in handling exotic birds. If the average citizen were to take that advice, both the eagle and the citizen could be put in harm's way," he cautioned.

After several other attempts at getting assistance, it was the experienced Reed who finally approached the eagles.

'I removed two of the four talons from the other bird's side. Then I picked both eagles up out of the ditch and moved them to a picnic table to finish the separation. This action was enough to make them want to separate on their own and fly 50 feet away, where they got their bearings and flew off in different directions," Reed reported.

"I feel very fortunate to have been involved with the rescue of two of our endangered national treasures," the ranger said. "But," he added, "something needs to be done to help educate the public and get information to them about what to do in situations like this. We're seeing eagles all the time now, and [trouble always] seems to happen on a Saturday or Sunday.

"The public needs emergency numbers to call. Something they can cut out and put on the refrigerator."

Having lived in Alaska, where the eagle population is not in the least threatened and numbers around 40,000, I'm no stranger to America's symbol.

Injured eagles.
Photo by Craig Koppie, U.S. Fish and Wildlife Service.

Traveling along the Marine Highway, a state ferry system connecting water-locked towns of Southeastern Alaska's fjords and archipelago, I'd look for snowballs in the towering spruce along the shoreline. Find the white dots in the trees and you'd discover the nesting spot of one of the eagles for which this frontier is so famous.

When I begin to feel soft and cuddly about the big bird that can weigh up to 15 pounds with a wing span of six or more feet, I remember my friend from Kenai, Peggy Arness, who watched an eagle sweep away a small dog, its leash dangling in the air:

"Be sure and watch the dogs," Arness warned. "The eagles can fly down and pick a dog up in a flash! We have seen them do that with a small cocker, and they tried to get our poodle. Anyway, keep your eyes out. The eagles are beautiful, but they are vicious on baby birds, ducks and dogs."

Just Right

Lots of forces have worked together to help the eagle make its comeback. In Bay Country, now it's our turn to support the eagle's return to sustainable numbers.

If Warren Heising's children grow up thinking of eagles as backyard birds, like youngsters in Alaska, it may mean we too are on a new frontier. It may also mean that we have learned the most important lesson about our national symbol: that the eagle's only natural enemy is us.

—March 26, 1998

UPDATE: 2021

Eagles have reclaimed Chesapeake Country—and all of Maryland—as their home. On any given day in 2021, 3,000 bald eagles are among us. Many Bay and water communities enjoy the company resident eagles. We see them not only soaring, revealed by their bright white heads and tails, but also on live nest-cams recording the birds' lifecycle from many a nest. But few communities are so lucky as writer M.L. Faunce's Bayside community, The Swans.

Sandra Olivetti Martin

New Bay Books publisher

Ariadne

- five -

Seasonal Reflections

August - September

August
Earth Journal
Pushed and Pulled at Summer's End

Dog days end early in August, at least by the calendar. Like time and tide, our thoughts can't help but turn, too. All in nature is pivoting, a rotation we'd notice if we weren't still busy having summer fun.

At the dock, sailing masts clank in the breeze, chanting a new tune. *School days, school days* goes the melody as waves lap. We can tune-out this wake-up call, of course, but nature won't let us ignore her. She insists, so we obey and observe.

Growing up, a brother's birthday on the seventh of the month always seemed to make me notice more than the cake and ice cream, set out on an old drafting table under the grape arbor or canopy of trees in the backyard. Dropping elm leaves were crisp underfoot. Nothing like the barrage that would fall later, but the tree first to leaf out in spring was first to shed its summer coat.

Butterflies beckoned us to come fly with them. Ripening grapes hung in clusters, the aroma intoxicating. An August party may be steeped in summer ways, but even kids like to move on when they notice things changing.

This time of year, Queen Anne's lace starts to lose its starch; black-eyed Susans wink more than beam. Grass bristles our bare feet. Dried to sweetness, the scent makes us drowsy. Rose hips swell even as new blooms form. Crepe myrtle spills and splashes across our lawns in great pink puffs. A cricket quartet, soft and incessant, fills the air and the brushy borders of our yards, a blend of one sound from many voices.

Is there any time of year when the wind is as soft as in August? Brushing our faces as we bike or jog or drive country roads, paddle or powerboat on the Bay, the air caresses: You've felt its touch. This after blistering heat and before first frost.

Finally, nettles in the Bay release their hold, and ferns fried from heat change color. In streams, the water's still tepid, what water there is. Noticing the change at the summer's end, we are both pushed and pulled.

Officially bound by Memorial Day at one end and Labor Day at the other, summer starts and ends are different as Darwin's finches. We are different, too. But before Labor Day, the true divide of summer and fall, in August there's still time for daydreams and a few vacation schemes. But with one eye on the clock, in our hearts, we are ready for what comes next, whatever that may be.

When once I lamented summer's end to a friend, she thought deeply and offered this: "Somehow I prefer a season of fruit to flowers."

Her comment gave me pause and my own thoughts. So that's why after biting into a crisp apple of a brand new crop near summer's end, you can't remember the dog days of August for the life of you.

—August 19, 1999

Reflection

Navigating Home

I've got the latest technology, but it's not what guides me. There's an old song of my parent's generation, "Show me the way to go home."

That song came to me the other night, driving my new car with its navigation system on, global positioning finely tuned. It was just me on the road, a darkened night screen guiding me along the faint shoreline of Chesapeake Bay. On the screen, a small icon glowed brightly, as would a lighthouse beacon, leading me home. Not mirrors, but today's technology at its best, guiding me in case I had no compass, no bearings.

Though I've traveled far and wide in my life —and lived for a time in Alaska —I've come to realize I have a reliable inner compass to guide me, honed by five generations of family rooted in this area. Frivolously, I've complained to my brother a time or two of going over the same tracks year after year, analogously to our father, who drove a streetcar for 40 years over the same routes through Washington, D.C., a job he loved and had no problem ever finding his way home from, across East Capitol Street from the Capital Transit car barn.

In contrast, my younger brother once described himself to me as a vagabond. A career in the Marine Corps and now corporate life makes him a citizen of the world, no different from many in the 21st century. It's a life of unparalleled opportunity and challenge, not without its sacrifices or rewards, with children being raised far from the home and roots he knew as a boy.

My brother visited here after the death of our sister-in-law, tended to family business and stood outside my home close by Chesapeake Bay, where our childhood dreams were made.

He took in a long, deep breath.

"I always feel like I'm at home when I'm in your house," he said.

That's when I realized those same tracks I've gone over and over, and sometimes lamented, made sense in the larger scheme of things. It's a connection to something as indefinable as the brackish scent of the Chesapeake that I breathe in when I stop to pick up my mail at the post office, then drive a mile more to home near the water's edge.

At the end of an evening, after a family gathering in my parent's day, my father, aunts and uncles would inevitably croon: "I had a little drink about an hour ago, and it went right to my head ... Show me the way to go home."

It's easy, of course, to find your way when you have a compass and your bearings. But you don't really need global positioning or an icon on a lighted screen when you have an internal compass to lead the way, a compass that has little to do with technology and everything to do with your own family history.

—November 30, 2006

September Earth Journal

Fall Colors Flame And Flicker

Sit long enough and the glories of Indian summer are yours. The scene outside my door (and yours) is a changing diorama of color as nature forges on to another season. Just when we need a change, color is now nature's gift for us.

Transitory visits by creatures small and smaller sweeten the pot. Some visitors are so fleeting that even a trip to the post office will postpone the chance meeting for perhaps another season.

Such is life, of course. We take our chances as busy days somehow grow into long lives where we snatch scene of the seasons and particles of poetry when and where we can. Which is how I glimpsed the American redstart I've never seen before in Maryland but often have in Maine, up in true warbler country.

The sparrow-sized redstart prefers wood, swamp and orchard, the essence of Bay Country once if not now. You, too, will recognize this diminutive warbler if you chance on one this fall: It's a glossy black with striking orange or salmon patches on wings and tail and white underside.

From my deck I watched its characteristic flutter of wings against a backdrop of a turning maple tree. For all the colorful swirling, the bird might have been a falling leaf. But this is not nature's camouflage, just nature's tribute to a painter's palette as autumn approaches.

The migration is in motion and this merry midget is just passing through to winter in states and countries to our warm south. How smart.

As the tupelo turns and the maples sugar-up, I caught just one act in the fleeting seasonal migration.

—September 24, 1998

Reflection

Little Sister

Big sister Joanne and
little sister Mary Louise. *Faunce family photo.*

Billed as an historic match-up, tennis phenoms Venus and Serena Williams squared off on prime time, the first sisters ever in a U.S. Open Final. This dueling was the ultimate in sibling rivalry for two who had traded points across the court before their ages reached double digits. No two sisters in memory have faced off so publicly, so personally, so professionally as the Williams sisters at center court in the cavernous new Arthur Ashe Arena.

Tennis great Chris Evert, who once played her sister in a lesser forum, remembered the occasion as so "filled with emotion and a sick feeling in my stomach that I just wanted to get off the court." If the Williams sisters, formidable as separate forces, experienced such feelings at their recent meeting, it was hard to detect.

In the end, Venus was said to have outpowered her little sister.

Most sisters don't play grand slams. But what is true for many sisters is that the relationship transcends the occasion. In sports, in school, in life.

Maybe I'm just a little sensitive these days. I lost my own sister recently, suddenly without warning, doing the most ordinary of tasks, on her way to the pharmacy. Her husband's prescription in hand, she suffered a massive heart attack. With a new first granddaughter just nine months old and so much in life still ahead, she left this world for one we know little of and can only dream about.

My sister and I had little in common with the Williams sisters save for the distance between our ages, about 21 months. At eight and nine, the Williams sisters sparred on the court. At eight and nine, my sister and I shared less vigorous sports, skating and jump rope. "I always want Serena to win," Venus said of her sister following her victory. "I'm the big sister. I make sure she has everything even if I don't have anything." Growing up, my big sister did that for me.

Two years ahead in school, she passed down more than her used books. I was mistakenly called Joanne by my sister's former teachers, but there was no mistaking our identities. Then, and until her death, she was a quiet force. My sister was not Serena, but she was serene, a reserve of calm when the world wasn't quite right—when I had forgotten my lunch, was kept after school, and decades later when we lost our mother.

Throughout her life, my sister Joanne made a difference to everyone she knew—without fanfare, without raising her voice. In a world that boasts confrontation and challenge, my sister gave a boost to family and friends, her children and her children's friends, her colleagues and her church friends by the sheer virtue of her smile, her words and her generous, gentle, unassuming self.

As her little sister, I did win.

—September 6, 2007

Rebecca T. Ruark Rises

Captain Wade Murphy's First-Person Story of Loss and Resurrection

O Captain! My Captain!
our fearful trip is done.

The ship has weather'd every rack,
the prize we sought is won

—Walt Whitman

Everybody knows by now that Maryland's oldest skipjack, the *Rebecca T. Ruark*, sank to the bottom of Chesapeake Bay near the mouth of the Choptank River a few weeks back.

The subsequent resurrection of the 113-year-old oyster-dredging sailboat we call a skipjack here on Chesapeake Bay has as much to do with friends as with fate and faith.

Here's the first person story of *Rebecca T. Ruark's* captain, Wade H. Murphy Jr., as he recounted it to a rapt audience at Captain Salem Avery House Museum in Shady Side on a recent night.

"I'd rather dredge than anything else," Murphy began, speaking to a standing-room-only crowd over coffee and dessert.

Wade H. Murphy Jr., owner and captain of the Rebecca T. Ruark. *Photo by M.L. Faunce.*

The captain has worked the water for 43 years, and his face, as red and shiny as a cooked crab, bears witness to the weather's will. For all those years, he's crabbed in summer's blistering heat and dredged for oysters in biting winter cold. In between, he's made a living chartering his fishing boat, Miss Kim, and captaining cruises on *Rebecca T. Ruark*.

It's all hard work, but none of it harder than dredging oysters under sail.

"It's hard, back-breaking work, and you don't make much money. If I didn't like sailing so much, I wouldn't do it," he said. "There's nothing prettier than harvesting oysters under sail when there's oysters to harvest and you've got a good boat and a good crew."

They'd had a pretty day that November 2, dredging about 70 bushels, a whopping harvest for our times. The day's work done, Murphy's three-man crew had lowered and reefed *Rebecca T. Ruark's* sails to get her ready for the next day's work. That's the custom,

Murphy explained, because it's easier to unreef a sail now than reef one later.

The seas churning up about 3pm that afternoon were not pretty. Never in 43 years had the wily old captain seen Chesapeake seas like those.

"It was the biggest sea I've ever seen in my life," Murphy said about the day winds were clocked at 60 mph and the *Rebecca T. Ruark* foundered in 20 feet of water, spilling both crew and all those oysters into the 50-odd degree waters of the November Bay.

The crowd held tight to his every word.

Going Down

Seas turned rough, very rough, the second day of the 1999 oyster season.

"We finished dredging, and it was kind of rainy, with 20-mph winds. I left the upper Choptank River at 3 o'clock, which is normal—and thank God, because it would have been dark and they probably couldn't have found us. I probably wouldn't have been here tonight.

"I quit earlier because it was bad weather. It was winds like 20- or 25-mph from the south. We were under power about two hours from Tilghman, and we had a lot of open water to go across to get home.

"The normal thing to do," Murphy explained, "would be to hurry home under sail. It doesn't matter. 40- to 45-mph winds are no problem to *Rebecca Ruark*," he said.

"So when you finish working in the protected waters, you pull your yawl boat up out of the water, because it will sink in a minute in rough waters."

A yawl boat, by the way, is the little motorized push-boat allowed by Maryland's odd law regulating oyster dredging to push the much larger skipjack to its oystering destination. In 1965, the law was loosened to allow yawl boats to push the skipjacks as they dredge on two days a week. The remaining days, they must dredge under sail.

"So you pull the yawl boat up, you put your sails up and you sail fair wind," Murphy continued.

"We hauled the yawl boat up, and we started sailing to Tilghman. I've done it hundreds of times in the last 40 years.

"I listened to the weather forecast. I never pay a bunch of attention to it, but I always check it because sometimes they can warn you of a storm. So I listened to the weather and the weatherman said, 15-, 20-, 25-mph winds from the south, rain, no heavy winds. In the lower Bay off Virginia waters, there's 40-mph, but no wind in the middle and upper Bay.

"So we started sailing home and right in the middle of the Choptank, the wind breezed up more. It went from 20 to 25 to 30 to 35.

"Then it was blowing like 40-mph.

"No problem. We were still on fair winds.

"Then it started blowing more, and they clocked it at 60-mph. We were still going okay—until it started blowing the sails away. My sails were only two years old. It blowed the sails away and it was like the biggest sea I've ever seen in my life. It was rougher than I've ever seen it in the Choptank.

"So the only thing to do now is anchor. Because if you keep going with those sails, you're going to be broadsided and you're going to get swamped.

"I dropped the anchor; the anchor held her head to the wind. Then it started breezing up more.

"She started diving her bow under. Sometimes there'd be water up on my forward deck up to my waist. My crew was scared to death.

No wonder. Many a Marylander takes to the water without ever having learned to swim. Two brothers made up part of the crew that day. One could barely swim; the second could not swim at all. "They'd been with me three years," said Murphy. "Now both those guys say they'll never spend another day on a skipjack."

Hands in motion as he talked, the captain swayed and rolled like he was still riding the deck of the *Rebecca T. Ruark*. But the captain, like his ancient

40 to 45 mile-an-hour winds
are no problem for *Rebecca T. Ruark*.
Photo by Wade H. Murphy Jr.

skipjack, knows something about survival. Equipped with old-fashioned instinct and a modern cellular phone, he called home.

"So I called my wife on my cellular phone and told her where I was and that I needed somebody to come tow me and get somebody out there as soon as she could," Murphy continued.

"So she went to see a couple of watermen right away and they started to come out. But in the meantime, the boat started taking on more water. The crew was so scared."

Murphy's eyes are small and intense, maybe from squinting all those years, sun-up to sunset, out in the wind and waves of the open Bay. Peering out from under a white peaked cap, he wears a look a little like Lucille Ball's look about which Desi Arnez used to say, "You've got that gleam in your eye." But Murphy's eyes grew serious as he recalled just how scared his crew was.

"I said, 'You've got to keep the water out of this boat. If not, she's going to sink. She's taking on water.' Now on the *Rebecca Ruark*, we have two 35-gallon pumps. I said, 'Keep the pumps running, and she'll be all right.'

"I didn't know they were so scared they weren't even checking the pumps.

"They said, 'The water is gaining over the pumps.'

"So I said, 'You'd better start bailing because if you don't bail, she's going to sink.' They couldn't even bail they were so scared.

"I got up there—of course she was anchored—and I bailed until I couldn't bail no more—without realizing the pumps weren't pumping."

Working frantically, Murphy kept his skipjack—the boat he calls a "good boat"—afloat until rescue arrived.

"The people got there, and they started towing us in. About two miles from Tilghman she just took so much water over the bow, she went down.

"It washed the life ring off before that happened. It blowed that off the boat, and all the life jackets were in the cabin. We had seven survival suits in the cabin, but I couldn't get to them. There was a life ring on top of the cabin and it got off a little distance.

"I couldn't believe she was going down. She started down and I thought she was going to come back, and she never did. And I got off of her.

"I made it to this life ring, and about that time, one of my crew, a big fat boy, popped up alongside me and grabbed the life ring, and I said, 'shoot!' "

Murphy knows about as much about showmanship as about captaining. At the image of the fat boy sharing a single life ring, laughter flows through his audience, breaking the tension.

"And it did hold us both up," Murphy continued.

"There was so many lines floating around, we had to get away from the boat so a boat could pick us out of the water.

"The other two guys were up front, holding to the rigging. The brother who couldn't swim at all held on to the boat when she was starting to go down.

"Again brother watermen came to the rescue.

"Thank God, they're good watermen," Murphy continued, seeming to shiver remembering the cold and wet.

"They were just waiting to get clearing, and the tide this night was 10 to 12 foot. When the rescue

Rebecca T. Ruark listing to starboard.
Photo courtesy of Wade H. Murphy Jr..

boat backed up to get these two boys off the bow, one of them grabbed the life ring that was thrown to him, and they brought him on the boat.

"The boy who couldn't swim was so scared he was holding on to the boat. They threw him a life ring and he wouldn't take it, he was so scared. They threw it to him again, and he wouldn't take it. The third time they were screaming, and finally they pulled him on the boat and I thought for sure he was going to get drownded."

That life was not all Murphy had had to worry about. The *Island Girl* had hauled *Rebecca T. Ruark* quite a way, but when she went down, the tip of Tilghman Island was still a distant blur.

"I can swim," Murphy confided after the mesmerized crowd had taken their story home from Captain Salem Avery House. "But not that far."

Coming Up

Once he and his men were safe, Murphy's mind turned to the plight of his boat. He bought the *Rebecca T. Ruark*, his second skipjack, in 1984, spending $80,000 to get her into working shape. Now his beloved boat, his investment and livelihood, lay beneath 20 feet of water. He had to get her back.

"We got into Tilghman and it blew so hard, we couldn't get back to the boat," Murphy continued. This was, he declared, "A freak wind in freak seas."

"The next day, I got two towing companies and we'd almost get her up but just couldn't get her high enough to pump her out. We did this till dark, and we had to give up."

Those were Murphy's lowest hours. A third-generation waterman, he'd kept the faith while others abandoned it. And he'd kept it pure.

Dredging under sail in 100-year-old wooden boats is not the only way to harvest oysters. But it is the hardest way.

When you're dredging oysters under sail, on a windless day you wouldn't even get expenses. The closest oyster bar to Tilghman is two hours, so if you got the crew to go on a sail day, you leave the dock at 5 o'clock. They leave their home at 4 o'clock, you get to the oyster bed at sun-up, 7 o'clock, and if there's still no wind, you sit there half a day, then you still got two hours home.

Now, he thought, it was all up. Even if he could get the weather to raise his boat, where would he get the money? One commercial estimate was a whopping $30,000.

But Captain Wade Murphy was not without friends.

"Well, they had a meeting that night, some kind of political meeting about something else, with a lot of people there. I have to give Levin [Captain Buddy] Harrison [of Harrison's Chesapeake House on Tilghman Island] credit. He told the people that this boat was sunk, and if she wasn't gotten up in a day or so, she was going to wash to the beach. 'This was the oldest boat in the Chesapeake and they ought to try and save it,' he said.

"They told me that within two hours, the governor okayed the crane to come from Baltimore."

Harrison's message leap-frogged from the Maryland Department of Business and Economic Development to the Governor's Office of Business Advocacy to the Maryland Port Administration.

"Once the Port Administration knew the clock was ticking, they moved as quickly as they could," said Maryland Department of Transportation spokesman Jack Cahalan. "Within hours, the decision had been made to assist and logistics worked out on how to assist."

Three days after the old *Rebecca T. Ruark* sank, the state committed "roughly $10,000 to $12,000" to Baltimore company Martin G. Imback, Inc. to raise her.

"So they left Baltimore that night, November 4, at 9 o'clock," Murphy continued. "The next morning at 6 o'clock, they went and raised the boat."

Divers secured the boat to the boom of a heavy-lift crane, which, Cahalan reported, "very slowly, very methodically and very carefully brought the *Rebecca Ruark* back to life."

"If it wasn't for that," said the skipjack's captain, "I don't know if we could have got her or not."

Standing on the bow of a sinking boat suddenly gives a person a new perspective. So, apparently, can seeing her rise again.

"Usually bureaucrats don't work that quick," declared Murphy, who, his tone suggested, had seen just about everything now.

"This is something that's got to be okayed by a lot of people. That's why I guess the *Rebecca Ruark* is so important to them. They did the job, and I'm thankful."

AFTERWORD

Time was, skipjacks dominated the oyster fleet working Chesapeake Bay. Murphy tells the story of that fleet as if he had seen it with his own eyes—as did his grandfather, who came to Tilghman Island and began a career as a waterman in the 1880s.

"In 1885, after they had 15 million bushels of oysters harvested, everybody wanted to go oystering. The state law said that you must have a sailboat to harvest oysters. So, in 1891, somebody designed the skipjack. With its flat bottom, straight sides and hard chine, any backyard boat builder could build a skipjack," Murphy said. As many as 600 were built to ply these waters and reap an amazing abundance of oysters.

Rebecca T. Ruark is an anomaly among her kind. Built in 1886, she is a round-chine boat, which makes her a rarity among rarities.

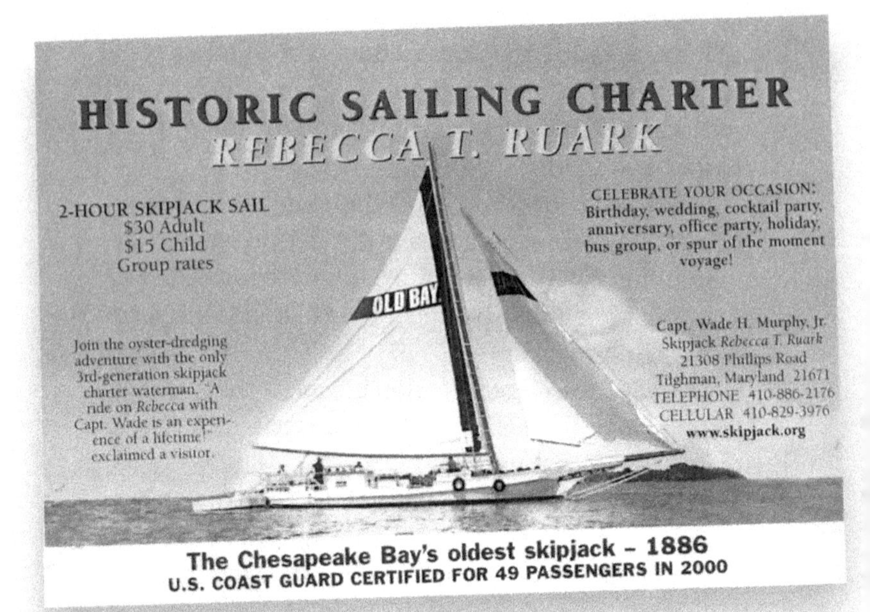

Postcard advertising the Rebecca T Ruark charter tours.
Photo courtesy of Wade H. Murphy Jr..

As we leave the 20th century, only 10 working skipjacks remain. That small Chesapeake fleet is America's last fleet at work under sail.

"So," said Murphy, "it's important to save this boat."

Rebecca T. Ruark's distinctive construction also makes her a piece of work when it comes to repairs.

"If she was a typical skipjack with straight sides, it would cost one-third the money to rebuild her," says the captain, who's now looking at a repair bill at least as big as the $80,000 he spent on initial repairs. More to do the job right—not just patch her up with glue and bailing wire, as has been so often done in *Rebecca T. Ruark*'s 113-year past.

"I could patch this boat up right now and go to work in a couple of weeks. And if it had been 20 years ago and I had babies home to feed, I wouldn't even hesitate," said Murphy. "We'd have got her up on Friday, we'd have worked till midnight Friday, Saturday and Sunday, and Monday and we'd have been sailing. We'd have just patched her up. And the next year, we'd patch her up again."

But this year—when the loss and recovery of the *Rebecca T. Ruark* coincides with the fleet's selection, by Maryland Commission for Celebration 2000, as Maryland's Treasure of the Month—is different.

"After you get so many patches," said Murphy, "you can't patch up some more. She's going to die.

"Instead of patching her up, I'm going to stay home this winter and get the boat fixed so maybe your children and grandchildren will be able to sail on the Rebecca."

—November 24, 1999

Skipjack fleet out dredging for oysters.
Photo courtesy of Wade H. Murphy Jr..

UPDATE: 2021

Captain Wade Murphy and *Rebecca T. Ruark* have aged together, an old couple who know each other well. Since her sinking and recovery in 1999, the old skipjack has held up well as can be expected for a 135-year-old wooden boat.

"I haven't had any problems, just small things to keep it updated," Captain Murphy texted. (In the age of Covid, that's the method of communication he prefers over trying to hear on phone calls).

He reports that he's been well, too.

The wild Chesapeake oyster, however, is not doing so well. Last year's catch of 270,000 bushels is middling nowadays, but a tenth of thirty years ago.

Selling in the Covid economy was as depressed as harvesting. "The market is no good for oysters," he wrote. "The restaurants are not open."

So he and Rebecca work as Chesapeake ambassadors to tourists, introducing them to the Bay, its oyster legacy and skipjacks, the sailboats that were the best oyster harvesters at the turn into the 20th century.

Skipjack tours were one of the many casualties of 2020, the year of Covid. Will 2021 let them back on the water? If it does, Captain Murphy is ready. "I'm planning on sailing again when the thing gets over," he wrote. "Hopefully it'll be April. I'll say I'll probably start May or June, hopefully ..."

Whether his hopes were justified, you, reader, may have already learned.

Sandra Olivetti Martin

New Bay Books publisher

ɔjack out dredging for oysters.
to courtesy of Wade H. Murphy Jr..

– six –

Seasonal Reflections

October – November

October
Earth Journal

Putting Summer Away

They say things happen in threes, but you and I know it's mostly twos going back as far as the Ark. The coupling is natural for most—not that all pairs work out. I think you know what I mean. Sure, some things come in ones, like hammocks, strung out between two trees, of course. Adirondack chairs seem to always come in twos—as a motif in pop art, on Hallmark cards, on the porches of fancy B&Bs, on lawns of cottages by the sea. Even the sturdy, unpainted wood models the Amish make come in pairs, together forever, connected by a little table between the two.

A pair of Adirondack chairs sat on my deck for a decade, side by side in summer sun, shifted sometimes to cool, leafy shade under Bay-loving gum and maple trees. A friend slipped into one once on a sultry summer day, body melting into the irresistible semi-reclining form and vowed never to leave. We've all made such promises at one time or another, and we mean what we say at the time.

Summer dreams are made in such chairs as the Adirondack. The very name conjures rustic settings and simple pleasures. Stretched out in this comfy perch, you can ignore children's antics. With only one eye open, spy a neighbor busy with chores. The bustle merely makes us drowsier and drowsier. In a semi-conscious state, you drift into the background noise, the clack-clack of locust and the drone of bees working hard on a patch of black-eyed Susies. Leaning back, gazing at treetops and clouds, we fix our only thoughts on icebox cookies and lemonade.

But now it's fall, and on my deck sits one Adirondack, ready to be put away for winter. If chairs had thoughts, they might wish for company. For while things often happen in threes and twos, they also happen in ones. I think you know what I mean.

—October 17, 2002

Reflection

For the Love of a Dog

Margo, a blind bullmastiff, has a human who prays to St. Francis for her every day. This seven-year-old, 134-pound caramel-colored dog is dearer than life itself, says her owner.

Sitka, the dachshund.
Photo courtesy Faunce family.

I met woman and dog at Anne Arundel Emergency Veterinary Clinic in Annapolis the day her human had brought her in for a suspected cancerous growth. "So unfair," says the human, for a pet that has already lost a fight for her sight to an infection caused by a tick bite.

The owner, who can't pinpoint the tick bite to either her home in Jamaica or Annapolis, where she's visiting, is not alone. Walk in any day (or night) at this 24-hour, 365-day emergency service, and you, too, will witness the boundless love that humans feel for their animals.

I made my first visit a few years back on my brother's 50th birthday. The party was over and my family was sitting back in the afterglow of a splendid celebration when my dachshund, Sitka, came waddling into the yard after helping herself to my neighbor's garbage. My brother and I dashed the dog to the Annapolis clinic, his small son in tow. Five-year-old Austin worried about this wiener dog because of his own recent stint at the doctor's office —to extract an M&M stuck up his nose. He could feel the little dog's pain.

Sitka was five years gone when I visited the clinic again this summer. My replacement dachshund, Rose, had become paralyzed after a daring dive off my deck. Two hours later, the patient underwent the knife to relieve a large herniated disc.

Biding my time in the waiting room, I leafed through albums set out on side tables. In the gloom of worry, I wished for young Austin's company and perspective. But in the albums, I found consolation in a letter from the grateful owners of Ratatouie, a sweet-looking black and tan dachshund, who praised the care given to their beloved pet.

Before Rose's explosive deck-flying accident, her life had been the stuff of backyard dreams: chasing squirrels and birds (to my chagrin), the occasional opossum, as well as targeting sunning snakes in the middle garden, meandering, marauding neighborhood cats, slow-gaited box turtles and feisty fox kits. All were Rose's playmates, including once a fence-leaping deer. All of life's pleasures were hers, including tamer walks to the Bayfront that beckoned a dachshund that didn't mind swimming.

Rose was a master of high jinks. Her military crawl would make Lassie weep.

Now, as Dr. Gray at Muddy Creek Animal Hospital put it, for a while "her little butt is shut down."

Americans will spend nearly $41 billion dollars on their pets this year, according to the American Pet Products Manufactures Association, with about $10 billion dollars for veterinary care.

My cousin, Carolyn, spent $9,000 searching for a cause and a cure of the ailments of her standard poodle, KoKo. My brother spent oodles before the discovery that his yellow lab, Cali, had Addison's disease. More will be spent to maintain the health of beloved family pets, yours and ours.

Dogs are famously known for their boundless love. But I've discovered the boundless love that humans —including veterinarians and young techs—give in return.

Pets are said to reduce health care costs for humans; they are often a great source of exercise as well as comfort and joy. People with pets visit the doctor less often and use less medication, according to the Humane Society. People with pets recover more quickly from illnesses. Still, we're probably not thinking of those stats when caring for our pets.

Rose is recovering well. In my house, dining-table side chairs are strewn across the sofa, a deterrent to high jumps. An ice-pink pet stroller awaits in the garage for walks to the Bay. Corrals and baby gates proliferate.

The vet says Rose will likely get back to normal. I don't know if she'll rise to chasing squirrels or birds, but I can hardly wait for the military crawl to begin.

November
Earth Journal
Between Seasons

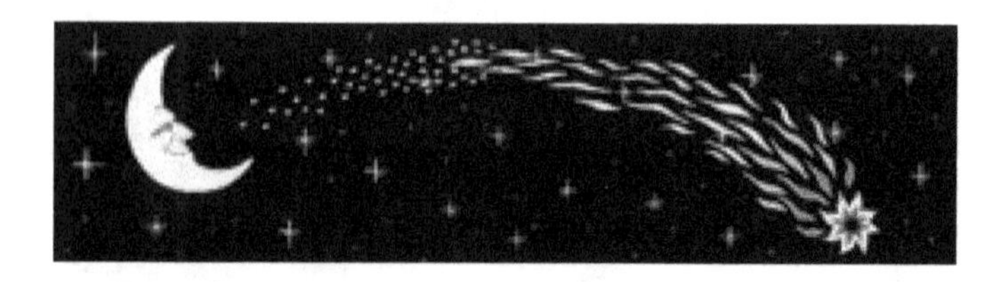

"I'd like to come back as M.L.'s dog," a friend of a friend said, a compliment, I suppose, for the well-traveled little pup in my life.

Watching this sweet dog lazily stretched out on a warm Indian summer day on a porch step in my yard, I couldn't help but think maybe we all should come back as some good dog owner's pet—this time of year, anyway.

I spied her watching intently as leaves floated from tree to ground, following each falling leaf as if it were the first, each time surprised, her twitching ears belying the peaceful body.

So it should be with us on this Indian summer day with Halloween's wondrous night now history for another year: carved pumpkins with their receding, puckering jaws, trails of candy squished by so many scampering costumed feet, the last remnants of the hallowed night.

No, now we'll rush pell-mell to the next seasonal affair on our calendars, marching to the drum of merchants and merchandise toward another Hallmark holiday even before the present one is over.

Study the pet in your life observing nature's show outside your window—leaves slip-sliding away, glorious color draining from our autumn world—a show so grand it should not to be missed. Observe the cat, all patience, in no hurry to be anywhere, waiting only for the chance to swat big, fat black flies that buzz between window and screens these days, seeking warmth but getting more than bargained for.

Taking the cue from my own pup, I stretched out on my deck that night, aware that we're living on borrowed time, a warm evening that can't be banked, must be spent now or else lost. Soon, I noticed streaks of light in the darkened sky and remembered the forecast for aurora, dancing lights seen most often in the skies of more northern lands.

When the streaks began to move, I leashed up my pup and headed for the shoreline of the Bay to get a better view.

Along the way, the Pied Piper in me shouted the news to neighbors just settling in for an after-dinner schnapps on their front porch. Not long after, three adults and two excited kids piled out of their car to the park along the Bay, they too cupping their hands to shield out the streetlight for a better view of the rare phenomenon. With ooos and ahhhs, we all watched in wonder until neighbor Mike noticed the regularity of the streaking lights and counted the intervals. "A searchlight," was his conclusion, and with no aurora, he returned to the car.

But by that time, neighbor Warren and his youngsters had noticed the moon in an early phase of a partial eclipse, which I later learned was predicted.

When I pointed out Mars, we began to notice all the wonders of a warm night in autumn beneath a cover of stars: The smooth ripple of the tide coming in bathed in moonlight. The softness of the air. The twinkling lights cast across Herring Bay from Holland Point, like some exotic seaport town burning bright. It was a moment, between holidays, when the world and we stood still for a little while, observing nature with the patience of a cat, the wonder of a dog. As if we had come back to life in some other form.

—November 13, 2003

Reflection

Thankful for Mashed Potatoes and More

Back during the Vietnam War, my brother served at a winter survival training camp perched on the side of Mt. Fuji, Japan, a U.S. Marine outpost out of firing range but not without serious duty. In his absence at Thanksgiving, my family thanked God for our blessings. I made a cassette tape of our family gathering to send to my brother; from my Dad, the eldest, to the youngest niece and nephew, we all sent our personal messages to my far-flung brother.

As we sat down to dinner, the tape rolled on, unbeknownst to us.

You think turkey is the starring role at this traditional feast? Or that stuffing is the stuff of our holiday dreams? The discourse on the mashed potatoes that continued during the meal became legend in our family. Once we tried to count how many times the words mashed potatoes were uttered, but we lost track in our laughter. Everyone had a personal take on the subject, and all repeating their words like rounds of a song. When one compliment faded in the background, another took up the resounding cord from the other end of the table. How creamy, how buttery! The chatter flowed on as forks tinkled on the plates like the music from the tickling of ivories on a piano. Nothing could still the tongue after tasting those potatoes.

On the tape, forever was captured the essence of the intimacy of a family meal made all at once special and mundane by the simple shared comfort of mashed potatoes. My brother still has that tape of the Thanksgiving when he was far away from family but with us in spirit.

When I moved to Churchton in 1991, having just lost my mother, I invited family and friends from far and wide for a Thanksgiving by the Bay. What better comfort, I thought, than to share the bounty of this quiet holiday with a walk to see tundra swans, to warm ourselves with oyster stew and, as the sun set, to eat and drink and share our considerable blessings.

The dinner table grew exponentially with the addition of card table after card table as invited and drop-in guests arrived. My Uncle George got tipsy and needed a handler; our two dachshunds got into a food fight under the table; my brother Pat's blessing took on a life all its own; the mashed potatoes grew cold, but no less appreciated—and I christened my new home and another era.

This is the first Thanksgiving since then that I will spend at home in Churchton. My older siblings have gone to heaven, and now their children will bring their children for Thanksgiving by the Bay. A nephew and his wife from California, and a Marine Corps family from Hawaii with young ones will walk and toddle to see tundra swans. My nephew John will follow in his father's footsteps and offer the blessing. Mashed potatoes will be on the menu. The rest as yet unwritten, a story for yet another time.

—November 24 2005

Magical Menageries

The Where and Were of Merry-Go-Rounds

On many a weekday, my brisk noontime walk on the Mall in Washington takes me back in time to a simpler period—at least in my life—of simpler pleasures. A block or so up from the high-tech world of the National Air and Space Museum, on the lawn of the Castle of the Smithsonian Institution, in good weather and bad, with or without joyful riders, the carousel whirls on.

My father called such wonders flying horses. Merry-go-round was the name we used growing up. A century before, wood carvers like the famous Gustaf Dentzel created fanciful horses and a menagerie of animals set on a platform with a center pole with attached cables, calling them simply "machines."

From the turn of the century to well into the 1950s and 1960s, these magic machines were the main attraction at the favorite playgrounds of middle class families, amusement parks like Chesapeake Beach Park and Montgomery County's Glen Echo Park. Many in the Washington area, like my family, have strong memories of both parks.

Most are gone now, and families have their fun at theme parks that make the amusement parks of my youth seem quaint and innocent. Chesapeake Beach Park locked its gates in 1972. But Glen Echo Park and its carousel live on, joyful relics of an earlier age.

Mildred Finlon rides the kangaroo on the restored Chesapeake Carousel at Watkins Regional Park in nearby Upper Marlboro, Maryland. *Photo courtesy of Mildred Finlon.*

When I recently learned that the National Park Service was seeking proposals for the commercial development of Glen Echo Park, I felt a twinge of nostalgia for the thriving "trolley park," the dazzling amusement rides and the exotically named Spanish Ballroom that drew the crowds. But most of all, for the carousel that captured our hearts.

Some 40 miles distant from each other, the carousels at Chesapeake Beach Park and Glen Echo Park had a special connection. Each park had two carousels in its history, and both surviving carousels were created by master carver Gustaf Dentzel. Both parks were connected to the city of Washington by rail line: the streetcar to Glen Echo and the Chesapeake Beach Railway to the Bay. Both had ballrooms that echoed with the big band sounds of Tommy and Jimmy Dorsey and Woody Herman. Each had a swimming pool: the unusual salt water pool overlooking the Bay at Chesapeake Beach and the famous Crystal Pool at Glen Echo, with a fountain and slides and its own quarter-acre sand beach.

The struggle for civil rights would overlap for both parks as well. The challenge of integration would close the gates to Glen Echo Park in 1968 (to reopen later under the federal National Park Service). Privately owned Chesapeake Beach Park would close for good in 1972.

But until those modern times, the old carousels turned many a happy round.

Carousel Facts

Carousel comes from the Italian *carosello*, or "little war" for contests of horsemanship in the 12th century.

Carousels imitate the French—and Maryland state—sport of jousting or ring piercing.

Early carousels were powered by man or horse drawn; they were mechanized after the Industrial Revolution.

Master wood carvers who created carousels in the U.S. were immigrants from Germany and other European countries.

Gustav Dentzel from Germany was first to turn the craft into a successful business in 1867 in Philadelphia. The Dentzel Company still operates today.

More great carvers with companies in the 1870s: Marcus Charles Illions, Charles Looff, Daniel Muller, Charles Dare, Charles Carmel, Charles W. Parker, Allan Herschell.

Each of the 12 major companies producing carousels between the late 1800s and 1920s developed a distinctive style — from the more realistic, elegant Dentzel figures to the fanciful and ornately decorated "Coney Island Style" of Charles Loof with animated poses, gold leaf and jewels.

The figures ranged from prancing horses to galloping pigs. Eighty percent of the figures were horses. Menagerie figures included commonplace roosters and exotic seahorses.

Of all the Dentzel characters, the rabbit and the cat were the most popular with riders.

All figures are hollow; all pieces were made separately.

Outer row animals were fancier; each inner row plainer and smaller.

Standers, horses and animals that didn't go up and down, were generally on the outside row.

Rollercoster Fortunes

Mildred Finlon, 88, remembers lying in her bed at night listening to the carousel music drifting over Chesapeake Bay.

Finlon came to Chesapeake Beach in 1922, when her father, a railroad dining car steward, bought property and eventually built six small cottages on nearby 15th Street. In those days, the carousel stood on a pier over the water.

That carousel was Chesapeake Beach's first, built by Gustav Dentzel himself in 1899, the golden age of carousels. Signing the contract for Dentzel's work was the visionary Otto Mears, who had paved the way to the Bay and its pleasures with his shortline railroad in 1900.

Fire destroyed that carousel in late 1926. "Carousel horses were thrown overboard," Finlon remembered, "and could be seen floating in the Bay."

Harriet Stout, the curator of the Chesapeake Beach Railroad Museum said second-hand legend confirms Finlon's first-hand recollection. According to the stories she's heard, for a few years after the fire the charred remains of the old carousel could be seen sticking out of the muck of the Bay.

Storms in the 1930s damaged the mile-long boardwalk and resort amusement rides built over the water, and the Depression led to the financial collapse of the railroad.

A new park named Seaside was later built on land. After the park was bought by new owners around 1929, another carousel of "mostly" Dentzel figures would be installed. It was housed in a building constructed just for it, placed on a hill overlooking the beach where with the ride came cooling, brackish breezes from the Bay.

It's that menagerie of carousel figures that several new generations—my own among them—would come to know and love at Chesapeake Beach.

During World War II, gas rationing did in the new park. In the war years, Finlon and her husband Harold lived in Washington, where she was a teacher and Harold worked for the Navy Department. They returned full time to Chesapeake Beach, Mildred's childhood home, in 1947. She taught school, becoming supervisor of Calvert County Schools.

When the park was revitalized again by new owners Wesley Stinnett, Joe O'Mara and the Cate Brothers of Baltimore after World War II, they found their manager in Mildred Finlon's husband, Harold.

Harold Finlon was born into a Pennsylvania amusement park family. He grew up at Glen Echo, where his father had taken a job designing the merry-go-round building and managing the park. In 1948, long after his boyhood days at Glen Echo, Finlon jumped from his job with the Navy Department to become superintendent of Chesapeake Beach Park, thus forging another link between the two distant parks.

Carousels on the Web

Tour the on-line Dentzel Carousel Heritage Museum, download the carousel coloring book, access the history of carousels from the 1800s to the present, see a census of all Dentzel carousels, including a few animals at home in Bay country—sea turtles, swan chariot, frog, deer and, of course, the Chesapeake Carousel's buffalo, goat and kangaroo. http://www.dentzel.com

Sharing management with Finlon was Stinnett's son-in-law Freddie Donovan, who had been a policeman in Washington. They made a "beautiful pair of managers," Finlon said, what with Harold's mechanical abilities and Freddie's law and business abilities.

"Harold could work on anything mechanical in the park—the pool, the rides, the slot machines—but the carousel and band organ were his first love," Finlon says of her husband. "No matter where he was in the park, he'd be subconsciously listening to the music of the carousel and would run back when the old Wurlitzer would miss a beat."

Two year-old Julie Shirley rides the pig at Glen Echo Park. *Photo courtesy of M.L. Faunce_*

EVERYBODY HAD A FAVORITE

In the days when the carousels turned, everybody had a favorite. For Gail Donovan Harkin, now of the Eastern Shore, it was the buffalo. "I still miss it," she said in an oral history with the Railway Museum at Chesapeake Beach. "You could never get enough of it."

Memorized by the generations as they picked and chose their favorites, the rings of animals went something like this: the innermost ring held the most unusual: a seahorse with its curling mermaid-like fish tail and two front hooves; the buffalo; an ostrich; a goat; and a burro. The outside "standing" horses were stationary sentinels going round and round but never up and down. That was reserved for the lively inside ring: the jumping kangaroo, prancing, star-gazing horses and a menagerie of other creatures.

A Carousel Primer: Books on Carousels

Carousels have become an endangered species. Learn a little about the language of the art, history and folklore to better appreciate this special craft by reading *The Pictorial History of the Carousel* by Fred Fried, said to have begun a renaissance by examining carousels as folk art.

"*The Great American Carousel*" by Tobin Fraley.

"*Carousel*" by Brian Wildsmith.

The kangaroo, said to have been carved by Dentzel himself, was Mildred Finlon's favored animal.

Actually, there were two kangaroos on the Chesapeake Carousel, which is how Mildred Finlon got plenty of time with her favorite. "Often Harold would bring one or the other home to repair the hinges in the legs," she remembers.

One of the kangaroos hung in her basement for nearly 25 years until the Chesapeake Beach Railway Museum was created. Faithfully and skillfully restored by Gary Jameson of North Beach, that kangaroo is now displayed at the Museum as one of the few tangible reminders of the beloved carousel that was sold in 1972. The second kangaroo still hops happily on the Chesapeake Carousel at its new home in Upper Marlboro.

Today, they may be the only two surviving jumping carousel kangaroos.

Carousel Time Capsules

Steve Crescenze, an industrial arts teacher at John Hansen Middle School in Waldorf, is a man after Harold Finlon's heart. This self-taught artist brings history back to life as he restores the antique carousel figures. He's restored over 150, including the buffalo Gail Donovan rode as a youngster at Chesapeake Beach.

"The buffalo is extremely rare," said Crescenze. "It may be the only buffalo made by the Dentzel Company." He's also restored a Dentzel goat for the carousel, and when I visited his workshop he was restoring a Dentzel-Muller horse—a "stander" with a double eagle on the back of the saddle—as well as working on a small brown inner row horse.

Crescenze doesn't have to ride carousel animals to get his kicks. Just getting up close and personal with these treasures—restoring standing horses, the celebrated buffalo or a beloved lion that resides in his home—seems to be reward enough.

Preparing the figures for restoration is exacting work Crescenze executes with caring hands. First, he strips away a small area to find the original colors. Then he strips the figure down to bare wood, which he repaints in bright original hues. Finally, he adds the "trappings": decorative details and finish work prominent on the figures that stood on the carousels' outside row but left off the unseen inside of figures.

Examining a finished product, Crescenze proclaimed himself "thrilled to work on pieces other craftsmen worked on so long ago and that will live on because they're being restored now."

He once found a message inside a lion's head. The artist had written his name and a few notes on the animal's construction and materials used.

"So now," Crescenze said, "I put in my own information and what I know about the origins. It's like a time capsule."

A capsule of that sort is precisely what Crescenze's house looks like. The man who used to restore old automobiles now lives with a menagerie that is part museum, part peaceable kingdom. On permanent display or in temporary residence for repair, at any given time you might find fantastic star-gazing horses, a massive lion, a clever cat with a fish in its mouth (facing in so as not to offend), an entire wall of carousel figures and painted rounding boards of pastoral scenes that were used with mirrors and light to decorate the carousel.

Crescenze has restored over 150 antique carousel figures, many from the Chesapeake Carousel.

"I love the painting; even the scraping is interesting. It's so exciting to see what you can find in the details covered up so long ago in so many layers of paint. There's so much art and history to this, it gives you chills," the craftsman said.

At the foot of Crescenze's bed stands a large park-size carousel horse he attributes to Charles Carmel, in the style of Charles Look, both famous woodcarvers. Decorated in the N.Y. Coney Island style and faithfully restored by Crescenze, it's in the right room for a dream ride.

THE THRILLS GO ON

The Chesapeake Carousel rides on. Twenty-five miles from its original home on the Bay, it still brings magic to visitors at Watkins Regional Park in nearby Upper Marlboro, Maryland. The debut at its new home in 1972 was made all the more welcome by panels depicting scenes of Prince George's county history, designed and painted by the Laurel Art Guild. Restoration of the carousel figures, begun by Rosa Ragan, continues by Steve Crescenze.

Last fall, I visited the park to take a ride on Gail Harkin's buffalo and met Mark Wakefield, 18, of Bowie, who was finishing up his second season as a carousel operator at Watkins Park. Operating the carousel "has been a lot of fun," Wakefield said. "You get to work with all different kinds of people; it's a good experience to work with kids, and it's nice to be outdoors."

When Steve Crescenze came to pick up two figures for restoration, Wakefield got a history lesson. He learned about the master carvers who had made these magnificent carousel figures. Of course Wakefield already knew their value: he could see that in the children's face as he rang the bell to signal the generous ride he gives.

Wakefield wasn't sure he'd be back in the summer of '98 to operate the carousel. Maybe that's why he so intently watched the figures go by: the seahorse, buffalo, ostrich, goat and burro. The unique kangaroo is working just fine, the rear-action hinged feet smoothly creating a jumping action.

As Wakefield began a new chapter of his life as a freshman at the University of Maryland, majoring in music education, no doubt a few tunes—like "Puff the Magic Dragon" and the Michigan fight song that he's heard over and over for two summers as the carousel whirled on—ran around in his head. Those and the "giggles and laughter of the kids."

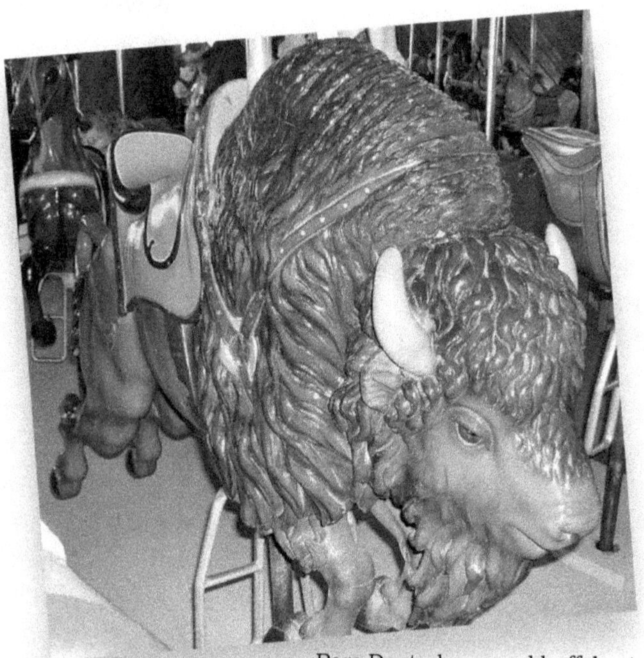

Rare Dentzel carousel buffalo at Watkins Regional Park in Upper Marlboro, Maryland. *Photo by Gary Nance*

Care and Feeding of Carousel Animals

Managers and operators still have to be able to work on all the mechanics of the carousel, Diane Baker, a manager at the park, told me. "We have to be a jack of all trades," she said. With all the other operators at Watkins Regional Park, Wakefield had to learn all about the carousel, the lights, the gears and the music, nowadays from three tapes played over and over.

Harold Finlon would have liked knowing that the people now caring for the old Chesapeake carousel still listen, no matter where they are in the park, for the carousel's voice.

The beloved Wurlitzer band organ that was once a part of the magic that drifted over the Chesapeake Bay has disappeared, no one knows where. But the carousel itself is well cared for.

"On Mondays, the ride is closed and each carousel figure is washed, with water, not soap," Wakefield explained. Slowly washing the figures seems a good way to appreciate the beauty and the history until they almost come alive.

Through two world wars and an intervening depression, the carousels at Chesapeake Beach Park and Glen Echo Park delighted and united young and old in a way few things in life can. But modern times tested their resilience, and 20 years ago interest reawakened just in time to rescue an endangered species. To today's enthusiasts who await the fate of Glen Echo Park, these are flying machines ready to take us back to the future. They are dream machines, still able to share with new children Mildred Finlon's "magic moments."

—May 14, 1998

UPDATE: 2021

Dentzel carousels at both Watkins Regional Park and Glen Echo Park are looking grand as new despite their longevity. The Chesapeake, created in 1905, will celebrate 50 years at Carousel at Watkins Regional Park in 1972. The Glen Echo carousel celebrates its centennial in 2021. The highly decorated dodecagonal—that's twelve-sided—pavilion enclosing the carousel was restored in 2019-2020. The roof

was replaced, original murals repainted and the room that holds the carousel organ—what's a merry-go-round without music?—restored. The organ itself, one of 12 surviving Wurlitzer band organs, was removed for refurbishment. Now all is ready for a year of celebration, likely to begin virtually. Covid-19 permitting, both carousels and their creatures will again revolve from May to September.

Sandra Olivetti Martin
New Bay Books publisher

- seven -

Seasonal Reflections

December

December
Earth Journal

Sometimes Wind and Sometimes Rain

My father loved to hear the rain on the roof. He said that sound, more than any other, made him sleep like a baby. But after five months of drought in Bay country, we haven't often had the pleasure of drifting off to sleep with the soothing song of a steady downfall. Now, we have to make do with another of nature's vibrations (and pray for rain).

The lullaby that lulls me to sleep is a drier, crisper sound. Here's the story it tells.

The leaves that fall at the end of autumn still cling tightly. Finally, the leaves yield to gravity as the wind strips the trees bare. Then the wind whips up, more proof we're on the cusp of winter.

The wind, spawned by the Bay like a bellows, rushes through the tallest loblolly like the fury of the ocean. Tenaciously, the leaves cling to the fullest oak, ready for the battle royal as a wind tunnel of colder air sets in. The sweet gum, too, puts up a fight, then succumbs big time to join the rush of flight between heaven and earth.

The change of seasons is seamless in nature's view, if not our own. We fight change, too.

Now is the time to listen for the sound of Nature's music in your ears. The crackle of leaves blows down the street—a whirling dervish of brittle foliage, much like a puppy chasing its tail till the blur is a grrrrrr.

Take a walk at night, and the swirling scene has a ghostly effect. Dry leaves rush helter-skelter past and around us. Lie in bed and it's a symphony. Trees sway and hum in the wind. Fallen leaves race across the ground and through the woods. The constant rush sounds like rain. But we know better.

The gardener in me longs to hear the soothing sound of rain on the roof, to nourish my dreams and the good earth outside. But at least we have the wind to remind us that nature is with us. Now, wrestling the leaves from the trees. Then paving the way for another season still far off, when surely, the rain will fall.

Sometimes wind and sometimes rain
Goodness, how we'd like to know
Why the weather alters so.

—November 26, 1998

Reflection

Phoning Home On a Starry Night

Thoughts large and small on a moonless night when all was calm, all was bright.

The millennium is fast approaching, but 2030 might just as well be light years away. That's the next time sky watchers will be treated to another a fantastic firestorm of meteoric fireworks like the Leonid meteor showers that just visited us.

Thanks to my fine-tuned hearing, I didn't miss a thing. They say other senses sharpen when one sense fails. My hearing has always been keen: I can even hear white noise. But for a while the other night, my hearing was dulled as a vaporizer droned on in my bedroom. I don't have a baby, just a bad cold. Tired of the background sound, I snapped off the machine and lay in my bed, hoping for a little sleep. In the quiet, I sensed movement outside and heard a subtle rattle and clack. It was exactly 4am.

Curious, I ventured out on the deck to find four wide eyes belonging to two startled raccoons staring back at me. Their hands were in the till—or rather, the bird feeder. Wide awake after shooing off the raccoons, I remembered the meteor showers.

The night was moonless: calm and bright. The Milky Way filled the heavens. Planets I've only dreamed of took their momentary positions. (Do you remember the difference? Stars twinkle, planets don't.) With bare feet on a cold deck in the middle of the night, I waited.

Oh, the celestial thoughts that came to me: My cousin Billy's room when we were small. The ceiling painted midnight blue and covered with stars. The Fourth Avenue Theater in Anchorage, Alaska, that ceiling memorable too. In the darkened theater, the Big Dipper cast its glow on the double seat in the balcony that teenage couples always scrambled for.

Night thoughts raced on. Crawling out of a camp tent along the Denali Highway, rubbing my eyes to be certain of the sight: the pulsating aurora illuminating the sky. My brother sitting at the window of my Bayview home, watching neighborhood activities on the Fourth of July: his last earthly fireworks. Now he owns the skies. Lying on the screen porch at my Aunt Mary's cottage on the Patuxent River and seeing falling stars. Only kids get to see falling stars.

Phoning home from Air Force I while winging my way north to Alaska on a night the pilot proclaimed, "visibility unlimited." Mom said, "your Dad's asleep in his chair." The next day, Dad told all his friends he talked to his daughter from aboard the president's plane.

A light comes on in the window of my neighbor Joe's house, signaling the end of the great balls of fire falling from the heavens. It's getting light. We won't see another meteor shower like this.

The truth is, I didn't see a single streaking meteor, much less a meteor storm. But I did think thoughts large and small on a moonless night when all was calm, all was bright. Maybe it was just my cold or my bare feet on the deck outside that brought on the need on that starry night to phone home to the store of heavenly memories that rest deep within all of us.

—November 26, 1998

The Author on Her Life

A fifth generation Washingtonian, I was born Mary Louise Faunce in 1944 in the District of Columbia, always referred to as "the District" back then, the third child of Florence L. and John Patrick Faunce. I was an outdoors girl, outside in any weather, climbing trees and telephone poles. All four Faunce children attended District parochial schools through high school.

My father was a streetcar driver. From our home on East Capitol Street, west to the U.S. Capitol, north to Union Station and on to Georgetown, birthplace of both my parents in a more modest era, his route traced family roots going back all those generations.

Senators and congressmen—at the time, all were mostly men—used public transportation back then. Boarding his streetcar, they called my father by name. The view of the U.S. Capitol from the windshield of the streetcar, framed by spreading elms, stays with me to this day, foretelling the connection to my future.

After high school, my sister and I were expected to find jobs; college was an option only for boys. In Washington in those days, government jobs abounded for young women. My sister, two years older, found her job at the State Department. I began work in 1962, just out of high school, as a secretary at NASA Headquarters Office of International Affairs in the heyday of space flights and astronaut world tours. NASA had a Paris office, where I was able to visit often during my six years with the space agency.

With travel, school at night and mentoring by the generous senior staff at NASA and State Department Foreign Service officers and their families, my education and my world grew. In 1968, caught up in the winds of politics and Vietnam War, I wrote to a newly elected U.S. Senator from Alaska and got the job: assistant to the Press Secretary. Thus began a 40-year career on Capitol Hill working mostly for Alaska members, traveling and living in Alaska.

For many years, my charge was Constituent Services, for in past times elected members took pride in helping their constituents whenever they had problems with the federal government. Whether the issue was Social Security or Medicare, immigration or the IRS or housing, we were ombudsmen for our constituents. For rural Alaskan communities only reached by water or plane, serving constituents was a challenge. Trust me: I have been there, once by dog team in the far north.

Beyond retirement, I worked for a Congressional Commission on China, still on the Capitol campus, until my second retirement in 2011. Amidst a busy working life, I preserved my lifelong passion for all things outdoors and for observing and writing about nature's precious gifts, microscopic and vast. That disposition and pleasure I learned from my Uncle George when I was a child combing the Chesapeake for sharks' teeth or prowling the banks of the Potomac River. He showed me how to see the shapes, their story, their place in the world—and to appreciate the moment.

I have appreciated a lifetime of moments not only in Chesapeake Country and Alaska but also summers in Maine at a lake cottage shared with friends, and now on the Gulf Coast of Florida on the smaller Boca Ciega Bay.

I have also enjoyed the company of life partners, friends and dachshunds.

So many gifts have I been given by so many in my life.

Photo Credits

CPSIA information can be obtained
at www.ICGtesting.com
Printed in the USA
FSHW021424010421
80006FS